# CUT AND CREATE!

## TRANSPORTATION

### EASY STEP-BY-STEP PROJECTS THAT TEACH SCISSOR SKILLS

**Written and illustrated by Kim Rankin**

## Teaching & Learning Company

1204 Buchanan St., P.O. Box 10
Carthage, IL 62321-0010

# This book belongs to

Cover by Kim Rankin

Copyright © 1997, Teaching & Learning Company

ISBN No. 1-57310-084-6

Printing No. 987654321

**Teaching & Learning Company**
**1204 Buchanan St., P.O. Box 10**
**Carthage, IL  62321-0010**

TLC10084 Copyright © Teaching & Learning Company, Carthage, IL  62321-0010

# TABLE OF CONTENTS

Shapes . . . . . . . . . . . . . . . . . . . . . . . . . . . . . . . . . . . . . . . . . . . . . .5

Suggestions for Using Some of the Projects . . . . . . . . . . . . . . .6

Airplane . . . . . . . . . . . . . . . . . . . . . . . . . . . . . . . . . . . . . . . . . . .7

Ambulance . . . . . . . . . . . . . . . . . . . . . . . . . . . . . . . . . . . . . . . .10

Ark . . . . . . . . . . . . . . . . . . . . . . . . . . . . . . . . . . . . . . . . . . . . . . .13

Bicycle . . . . . . . . . . . . . . . . . . . . . . . . . . . . . . . . . . . . . . . . . . .15

Bulldozer . . . . . . . . . . . . . . . . . . . . . . . . . . . . . . . . . . . . . . . . .17

Car Side View . . . . . . . . . . . . . . . . . . . . . . . . . . . . . . . . . . . . . .20

Car Front View . . . . . . . . . . . . . . . . . . . . . . . . . . . . . . . . . . . . .22

Combine . . . . . . . . . . . . . . . . . . . . . . . . . . . . . . . . . . . . . . . . . .25

Crane . . . . . . . . . . . . . . . . . . . . . . . . . . . . . . . . . . . . . . . . . . . .28

Dump Truck . . . . . . . . . . . . . . . . . . . . . . . . . . . . . . . . . . . . . . .31

Fire Truck . . . . . . . . . . . . . . . . . . . . . . . . . . . . . . . . . . . . . . . . .34

Gas Truck . . . . . . . . . . . . . . . . . . . . . . . . . . . . . . . . . . . . . . . . .37

Helicopter . . . . . . . . . . . . . . . . . . . . . . . . . . . . . . . . . . . . . . . . .40

Loader . . . . . . . . . . . . . . . . . . . . . . . . . . . . . . . . . . . . . . . . . . .43

Mail Truck . . . . . . . . . . . . . . . . . . . . . . . . . . . . . . . . . . . . . . . . .46

Milk Truck . . . . . . . . . . . . . . . . . . . . . . . . . . . . . . . . . . . . . . . . .49

Mixer Truck . . . . . . . . . . . . . . . . . . . . . . . . . . . . . . . . . . . . . . . .52

Pickup Truck . . . . . . . . . . . . . . . . . . . . . . . . . . . . . . . . . . . . . . .55

Sailboat . . . . . . . . . . . . . . . . . . . . . . . . . . . . . . . . . . . . . . . . . .57

School Bus . . . . . . . . . . . . . . . . . . . . . . . . . . . . . . . . . . . . . . . .60

Tractor . . . . . . . . . . . . . . . . . . . . . . . . . . . . . . . . . . . . . . . . . . .63

Train . . . . . . . . . . . . . . . . . . . . . . . . . . . . . . . . . . . . . . . . . . . . .66

Train Boxcar . . . . . . . . . . . . . . . . . . . . . . . . . . . . . . . . . . . . . . .69

Train Caboose . . . . . . . . . . . . . . . . . . . . . . . . . . . . . . . . . . . . .71

Train Fuel Tank . . . . . . . . . . . . . . . . . . . . . . . . . . . . . . . . . . . . .74

Wagon . . . . . . . . . . . . . . . . . . . . . . . . . . . . . . . . . . . . . . . . . . .76

Signs . . . . . . . . . . . . . . . . . . . . . . . . . . . . . . . . . . . . . . . . . . . .78

TLC10084 Copyright © Teaching & Learning Company, Carthage, IL 62321-0010

## Dear Teacher or Parent,

"I did it myself" is a phrase which can be the foundation for a lifetime of accomplishment and positive self-esteem.

*Cut and Create* activities can be used by the teacher or parent to develop a variety of important early skills and to provide projects in which children can take pride and succeed.

- Simple patterns and easy, step-by-step directions develop scissor skills and give practice in visual-motor coordination. The scissor rating system in the upper right-hand corner on the first page of each project quickly identifies the easiest projects (✂), moderate (✂ ✂) and challenging (✂ ✂ ✂).
- Materials used are inexpensive and readily available.
- Finished products are fun, colorful and have myriad uses from play items to props; room decorations for walls, bulletin boards or mobiles; learning center manipulatives for counting, sorting, classifying or labeling; gifts or favors for parties or guests; and much more.

The simple and fun activities included in this book will help young learners build a solid base for a variety of skills such as: following directions, observation, discrimination and information processing. A variety of learning styles is addressed including visual, auditory and tactile.

Your art program, whether structured or serendipitous can benefit from these simple and sequenced scissor skill activities. You students will

- develop manual dexterity
- communicate
- learn to control his or her environment by being responsible for tools and materials
- observe
- discriminate (by color, shape, texture)
- sort, order, group and engage in other math processes
- imagine!

We hope you and your students will enjoy these projects. They have been designed to stimulate learning and creativity in a way that is simple and fun. So go cut and create! And have a good time!

Sincerely,

*Kim*

Kim Rankin

# SHAPES

Shapes are seen and used in everyday life. You can find them on street signs, houses, windows and rooftops. Notice the shape of a box of crackers, the crackers and a plate. Look at books, desks, floor tiles and shelves. The patterns in this book utilize many basic shapes and reinforce familiarity with their forms and names.

 **Circle** is round or the shape of a plate.

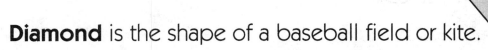 **Diamond** is the shape of a baseball field or kite.

 **Heart** is a popular shape at Valentine's Day.

**Octagon** is the shape of a stop sign.

 **Oval** is the shape of an egg.

 **Rectangle** is the shape of a door.

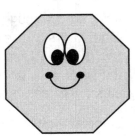 **Stars** may have many points. This star has five points.

 **Square** is the shape of a saltine cracker.

 **Teardrop** is the shape of a raindrop.

 **Triangle** is the shape of a roof on a house.

# Suggestions for Using Some of the Projects

## Different Uses

- Mobiles
- Tabletop or Desk Decorations
- Party Favors
- Take-Homes for Parents
- Refrigerator Magnets (Reduce 25-40%)
- Ceiling Decorations
- Window/Door Decorations
- Greeting Cards (Reduce 30-40%)
- Portfolio Pieces
- Folders (Reduce 30-50%)

## Greeting Cards

Celebrate a holiday or create an occasion. Handmade greeting cards are a surefire hit for parents, grandparents, relatives and friends. And what better way to say "thank you" to a visitor, custodian, principal, helper, etc.

## Mobiles

Here are two suggestions for making a mobile. One way is to use a sturdy paper plate for the top piece. Punch holes around the outer edge of the plate. Use string or yarn in random lengths to attach the ready-made patterns to the top piece.

Another way is the use sturdy tagboard. Cut a rectangle shape approximately 3" x 32" (8 x 56 cm) and staple the ends together to form a circle. Punch holes around the bottom edge. Use string or yarn in random lengths to attach the ready-made patterns. (Note: You will have to reduce the patterns 40 to 50 % so they are not too big for the mobile.)

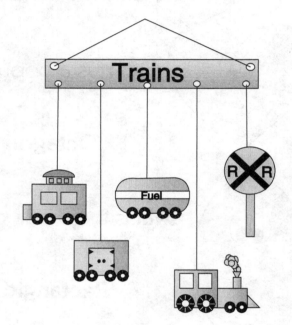

## Bulletin Boards

Make a transportation bulletin board. Use adding machine tape to create roadways. Add construction paper buildings, trees and landmarks.

Create two of each vehicle, make them mirror images. Paste to either side of a shoe box or empty milk carton.

**Materials:** *black, blue, gray and white paper; scissors; glue; black crayon or marker*

# AIRPLANE

**1** Cut one #1 plane from blue paper. (Note: Your plane can be any color you choose.)

**2** Cut one #2 window from white paper and glue as shown.

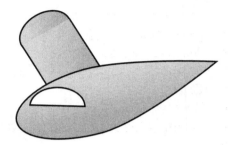

**3** Cut two #3 wings from blue paper.

**4** Glue a wing on each side of #1.

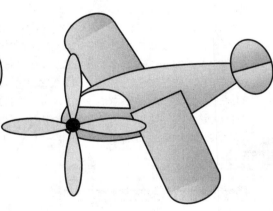

**5** Cut two #4 tail wings from blue paper and glue on the back of the plane.

**6** Cut four #5 propellers from gray paper and glue on the front as shown. Cut one #6 propeller nose from black paper and glue in the center of the propellers.

# AIRPLANE PATTERNS

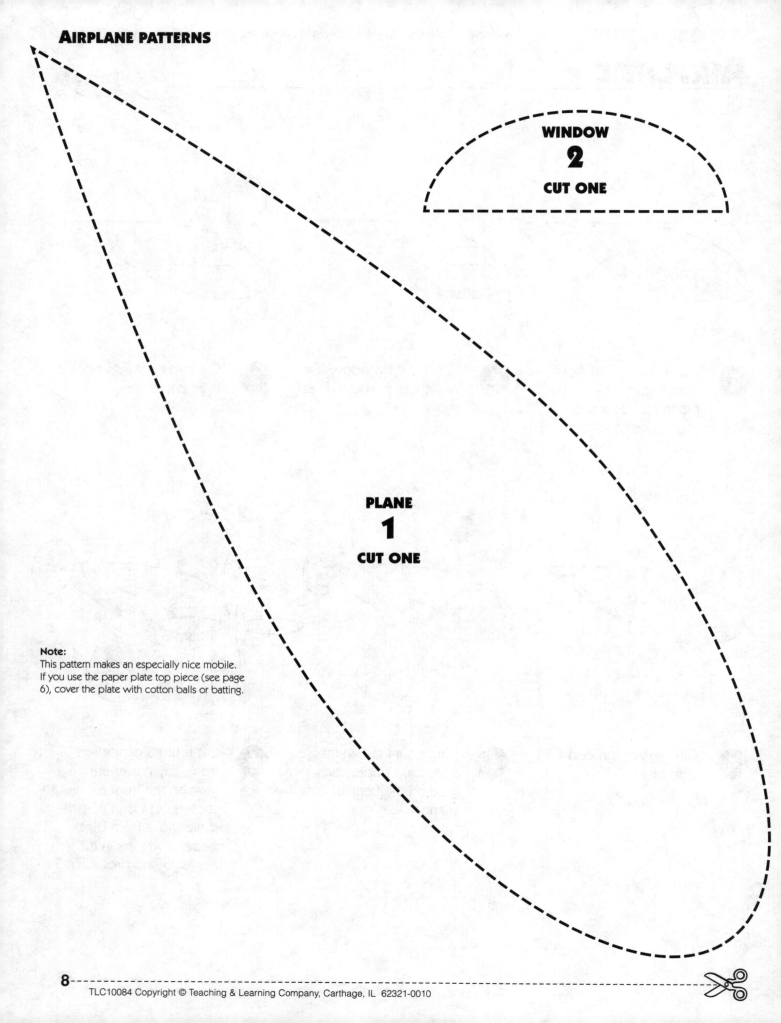

WINDOW
**2**
CUT ONE

PLANE
**1**
CUT ONE

**Note:**
This pattern makes an especially nice mobile.
If you use the paper plate top piece (see page
6), cover the plate with cotton balls or batting.

# AIRPLANE PATTERNS

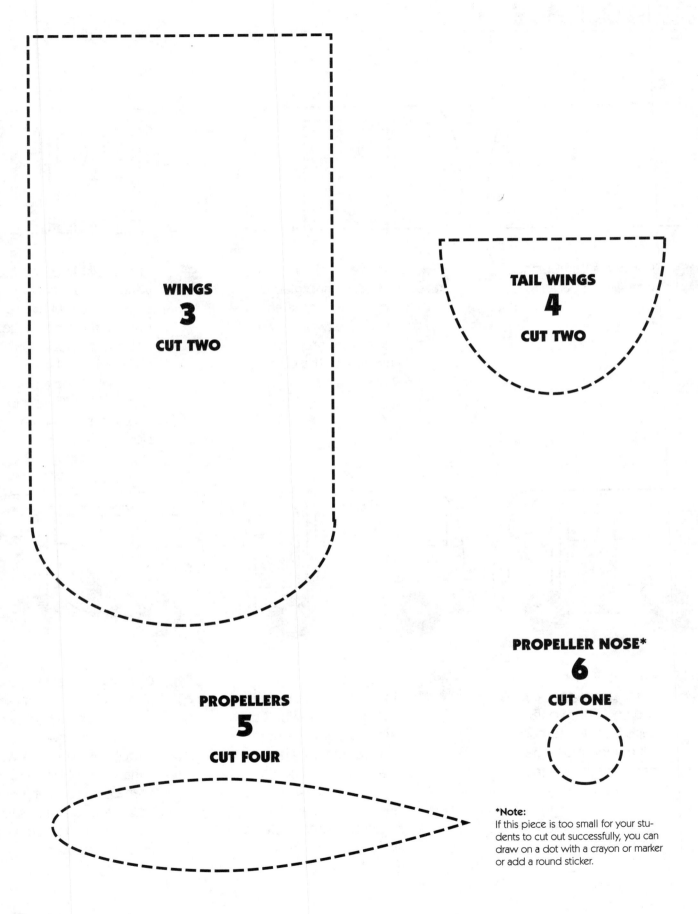

**WINGS**
**3**
CUT TWO

**TAIL WINGS**
**4**
CUT TWO

**PROPELLERS**
**5**
CUT FOUR

**PROPELLER NOSE***
**6**
CUT ONE

*Note:
If this piece is too small for your students to cut out successfully, you can draw on a dot with a crayon or marker or add a round sticker.

**Materials:** black, gray, red and white paper; scissors; glue; black crayon or marker

# AMBULANCE

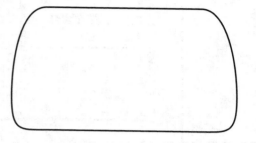

**1** Cut one #1 ambulance from white paper.

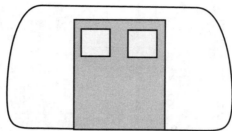

**2** Cut one #2 doors from red paper and glue to the middle of the ambulance. Cut two #3 windows from gray paper and glue to the doors as shown.

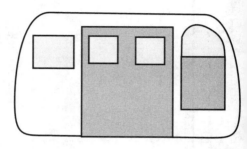

**3** Cut one #4 and one #5 window from gray paper. Glue #4 to the back of the ambulance. Cut one #6 door from red paper and glue to the front of the ambulance. Glue #5 window on the top of the #6 door.

**4** Cut two #7 wheels from black paper and glue as shown. Cut two #8 hubcaps from white paper. Glue hubcaps in the center of the wheels.

**5** Cut one # 9 circle for door from white paper and glue as shown. Cut two #10 bumpers from gray paper and glue one to the front and one to the back of the ambulance. Cut one #11 headlight from white paper and glue to the front of the vehicle.

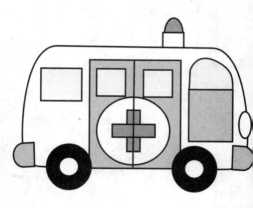

**6** Cut two #12 rectangles from red paper to make the cross on the door. Draw a line down the middle of the doors with a marker. Cut one #13 siren base from white paper and one #14 siren light from red paper and glue to the top of the ambulance.

**AMBULANCE PATTERNS**

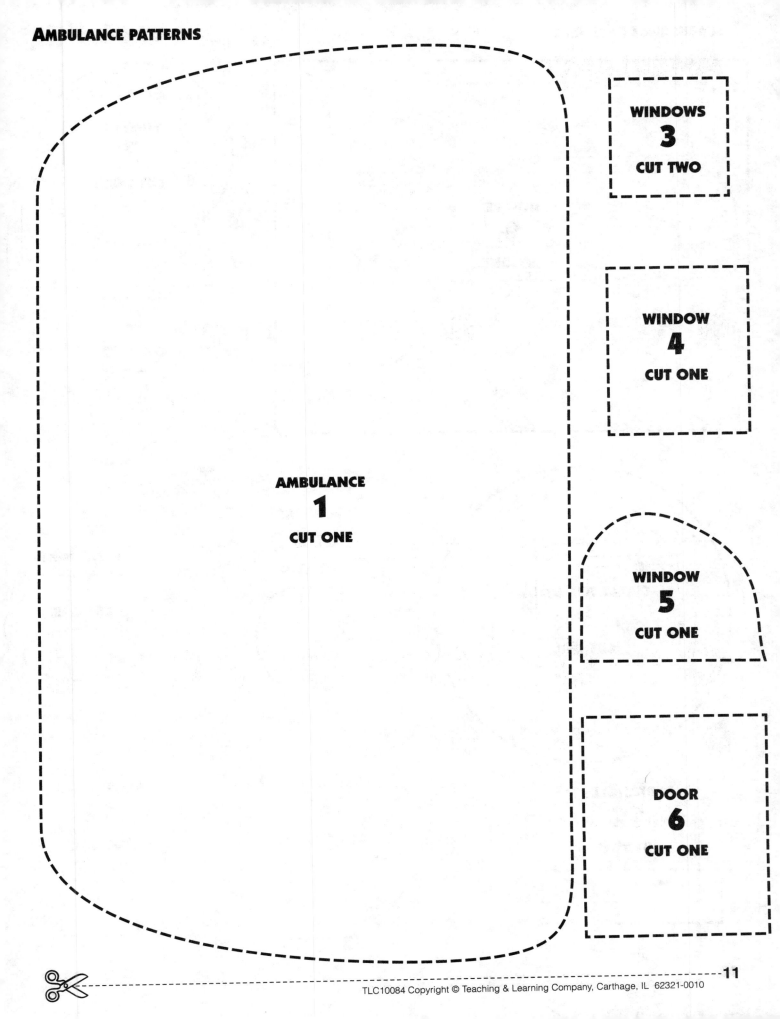

WINDOWS
**3**
CUT TWO

WINDOW
**4**
CUT ONE

AMBULANCE
**1**
CUT ONE

WINDOW
**5**
CUT ONE

DOOR
**6**
CUT ONE

# AMBULANCE PATTERNS

**DOORS**
## 2
**CUT ONE**

**WHEELS**
## 7
**CUT TWO**

**HUBCAPS**
## 8
**CUT TWO**

**Note:**
You could use round white or gray stickers for the hubcaps.

**CIRCLE FOR DOOR**
## 9
**CUT ONE**

**BUMPERS**
## 10
**CUT TWO**

**HEADLIGHT**
## 11
**CUT ONE**

**RECTANGLES**
## 12
**CUT TWO**

**SIREN BASE**
## 13
**CUT ONE**

**SIREN LIGHT**
## 14
**CUT ONE**

# ARK

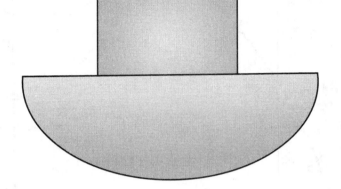

**1** Cut one #1 ark from tan paper.

**2** Cut one #2 cabin from tan paper and glue to the back side of the ark as shown.

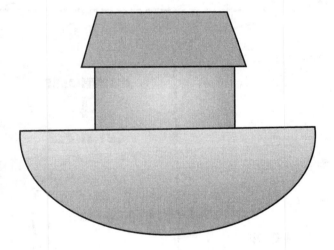

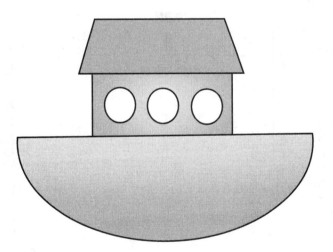

**3** Cut one #3 roof from brown paper and glue on top of the cabin.

**4** Cut three #4 portholes from white paper and glue as shown.

**Note:** Children can draw people or animal faces in the portholes, or decorate their arks with stickers.

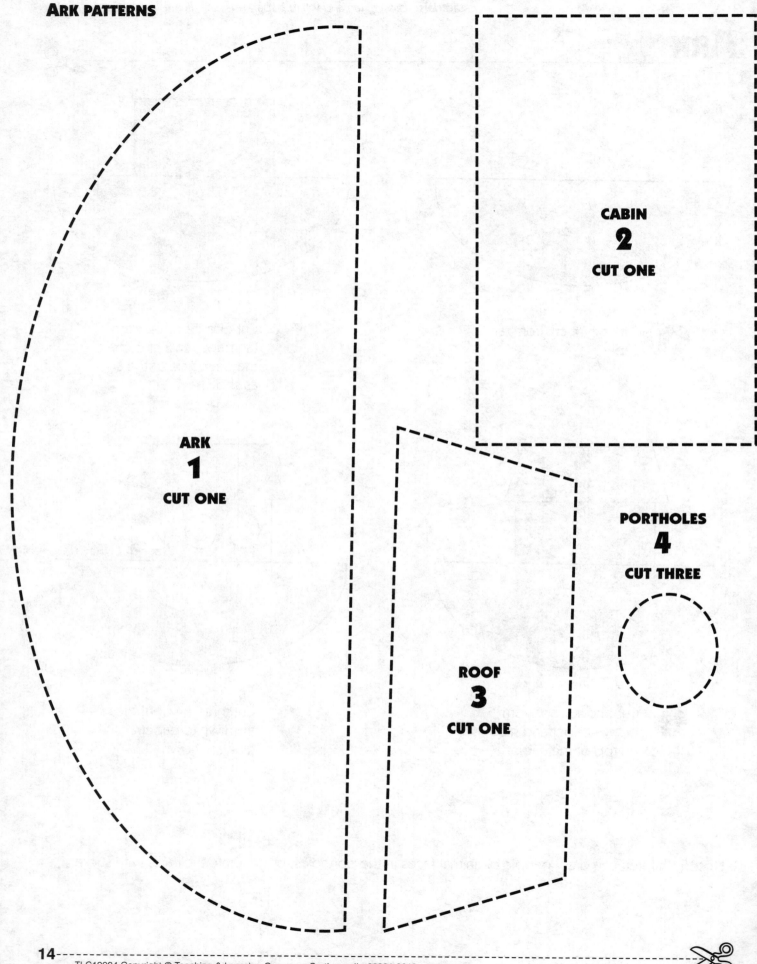

ARK
**1**
CUT ONE

CABIN
**2**
CUT ONE

ROOF
**3**
CUT ONE

PORTHOLES
**4**
CUT THREE

# BICYCLE

front

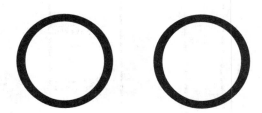

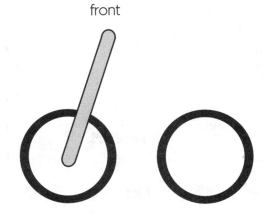

**1** Cut two #1 wheels from black paper. Cut two #2 wheels from white paper. Glue the white circle on top of the black circle to form two tires. Place tires side by side.

**2** Cut one #3 bar from red paper for the front of the bike. Glue to the front wheel as shown. Cut four #4 bars from red paper for the rest of the bike. (Note: You can use any color you want for the bike.)

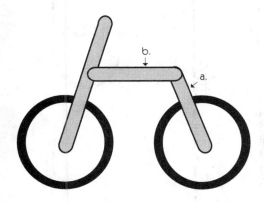

**3** Glue one #4 bar to the back wheel (a). Glue another #4 bar to connect front and back bars (b).

**4** Glue on two more #4 bars to form a triangle in the center of the bike.

**5** Cut one #5 handlebars and one #6 seat from black paper. Glue as shown.

**Note:** This makes a nice folder decoration for information collected on bicycle safety during National Bike Month in May.

TLC10084 Copyright © Teaching & Learning Company, Carthage, IL 62321-0010

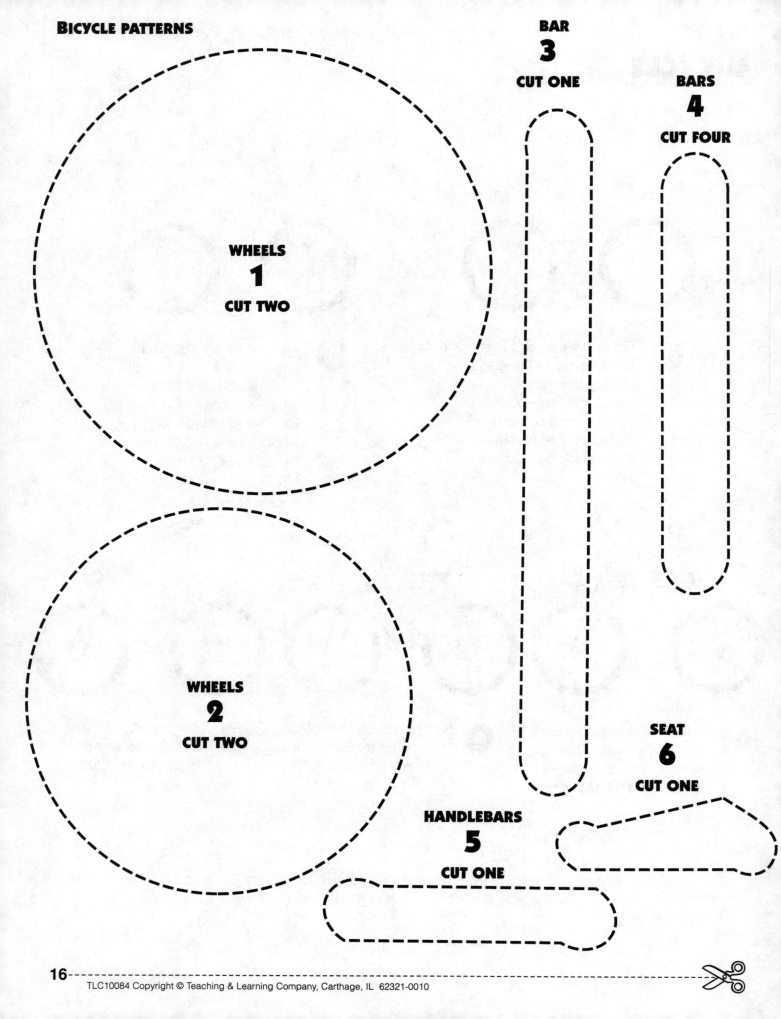

BICYCLE PATTERNS

BAR
**3**
CUT ONE

BARS
**4**
CUT FOUR

WHEELS
**1**
CUT TWO

WHEELS
**2**
CUT TWO

SEAT
**6**
CUT ONE

HANDLEBARS
**5**
CUT ONE

# BULLDOZER

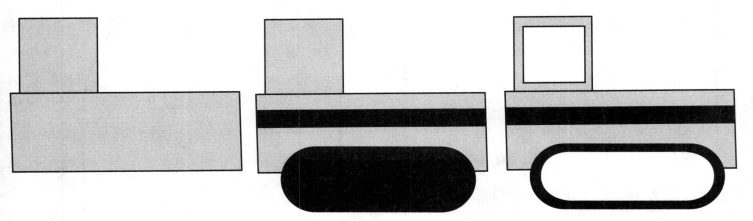

**1** Cut one #1 body from yellow paper. Cut one #2 cab and glue to the back of the body.

**2** Cut one #3 track and one #4 stripe from black paper and glue in place as shown.

**3** Cut one #5 track and #6 window from white paper and glue as shown.

**4** Cut two #7 wheels from yellow or gray paper and glue on each end of the white track. Cut one #8 lift cylinder from yellow paper.

**5** Cut one #9 blade from yellow paper and glue to the lift cylinder. Cut one #10 muffler from gray or black paper and glue in place.

# BULLDOZER PATTERNS

BODY
**1**
CUT ONE

TRACK
**3**
CUT ONE

**BULLDOZER PATTERNS**

**CAB**
**2**
**CUT ONE**

**STRIPE**
**4**
**CUT ONE**

**TRACK**
**5**
**CUT ONE**

**LIFT CYLINDER**
**8**
**CUT ONE**

**WHEELS**
**7**
**CUT TWO**

**MUFFLER**
**10**
**CUT ONE**

**BLADE**
**9**
**CUT ONE**

**WINDOW**
**6**
**CUT ONE**

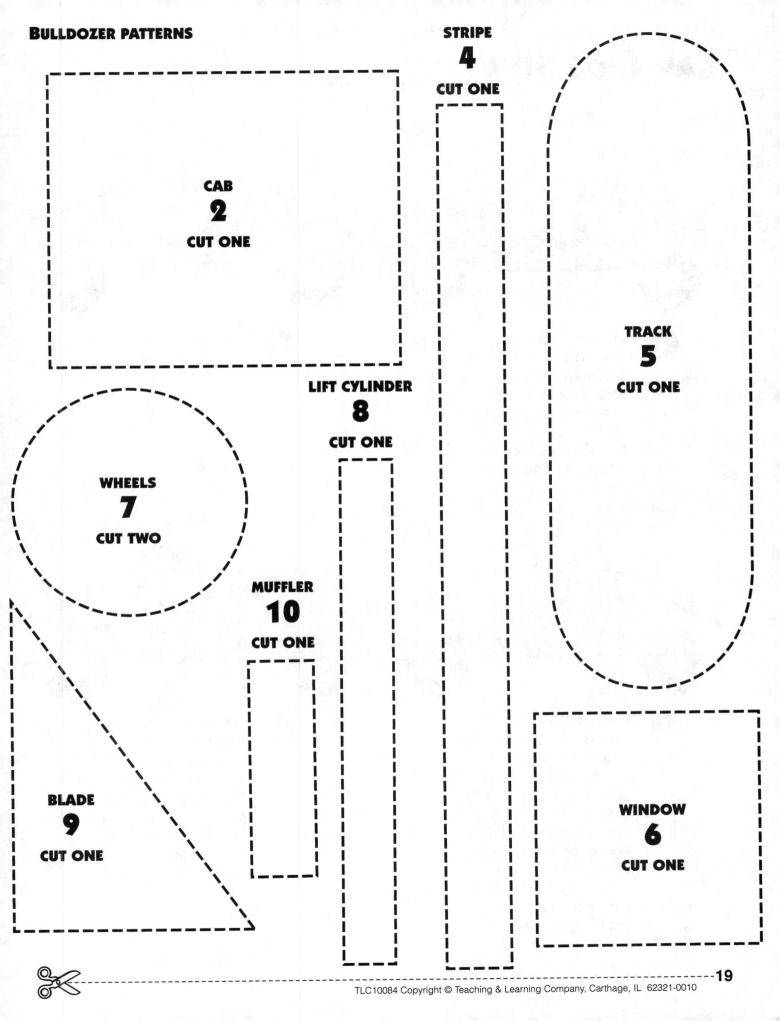

**Materials:** *black, blue and white paper, scissors; glue; black crayon or marker*

# CAR SIDE VIEW

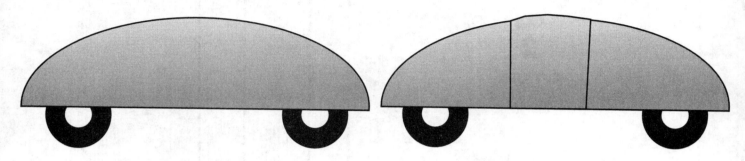

**1** Cut one #1 car from blue* paper. Cut two #2 tires from black paper and two #3 hubcaps from white paper. Glue each hubcap on top of a tire. Glue the tires to the back side of the car as shown.

*Children can choose their favorite colors.

**2** Cut one #4 door from blue paper. Glue in place as shown.

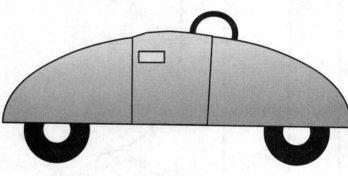

**3** Cut one #5 steering wheel from black paper and one #6 steering wheel from white paper. Glue the white circle on top of the black circle. Position slightly behind the car just above the forward edge of the door. Glue in place. Cut one #7 door handle from white or blue paper. Glue in place.

**4** Cut one #8 windshield from white paper and glue as shown. Cut two #9 wheel covers from blue paper. These are glued on above the tires. Cut one #10 headlight from white paper and glue to the front of the car.

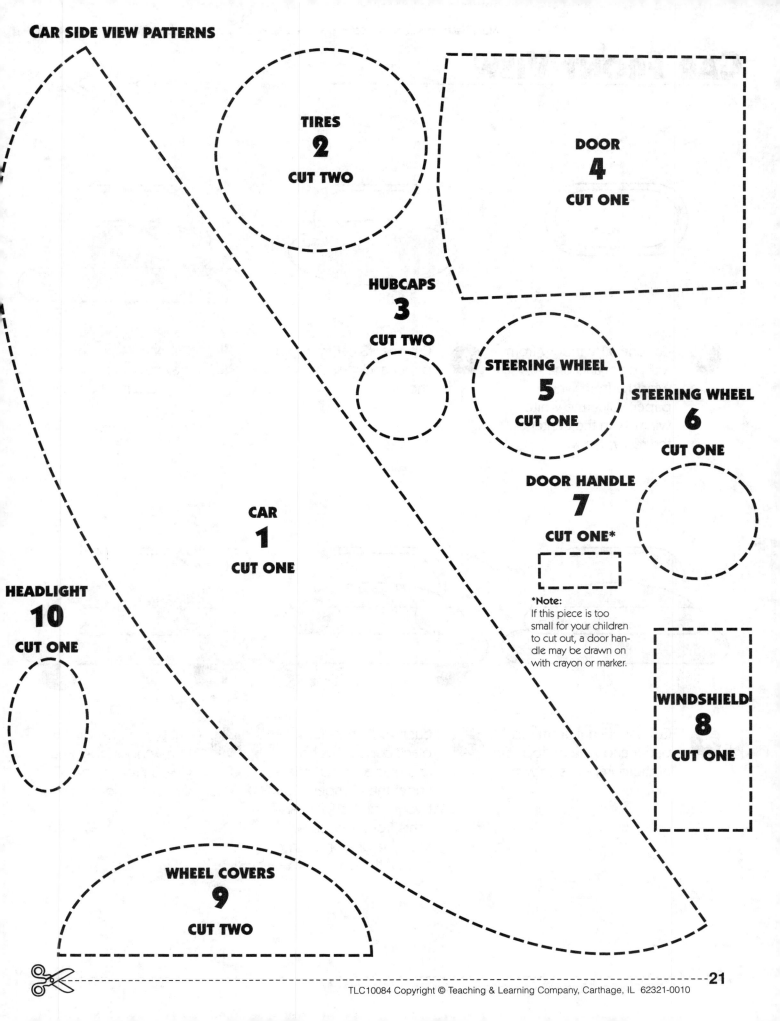

CAR SIDE VIEW PATTERNS

TIRES
2
CUT TWO

DOOR
4
CUT ONE

HUBCAPS
3
CUT TWO

STEERING WHEEL
5
CUT ONE

STEERING WHEEL
6
CUT ONE

DOOR HANDLE
7
CUT ONE*

CAR
1
CUT ONE

*Note:
If this piece is too small for your children to cut out, a door handle may be drawn on with crayon or marker.

HEADLIGHT
10
CUT ONE

WINDSHIELD
8
CUT ONE

WHEEL COVERS
9
CUT TWO

**Materials:** *black, gray, red and white paper; scissors; glue; black crayon or marker*

# CAR FRONT VIEW

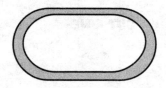

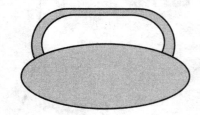

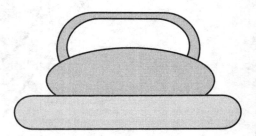

**1** Cut one #1 window from red paper and one #2 window from white paper. Glue the white window in the center of the red window.

**2** Cut one #3 car from red paper and glue as shown.

**3** Cut one #4 bumper from gray paper and glue to the bottom of the car.

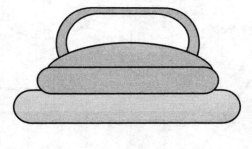

**4** Cut one #5 grill from red paper and glue on top of the bumper as shown.

**5** Cut two #6 tires from black paper. Position and glue at either side under the bumper. Cut two #7 circles for headlights from gray paper and glue one on each side of the car.

**6** Cut two #8 headlights from white paper and glue on top of the #7 circles as shown.

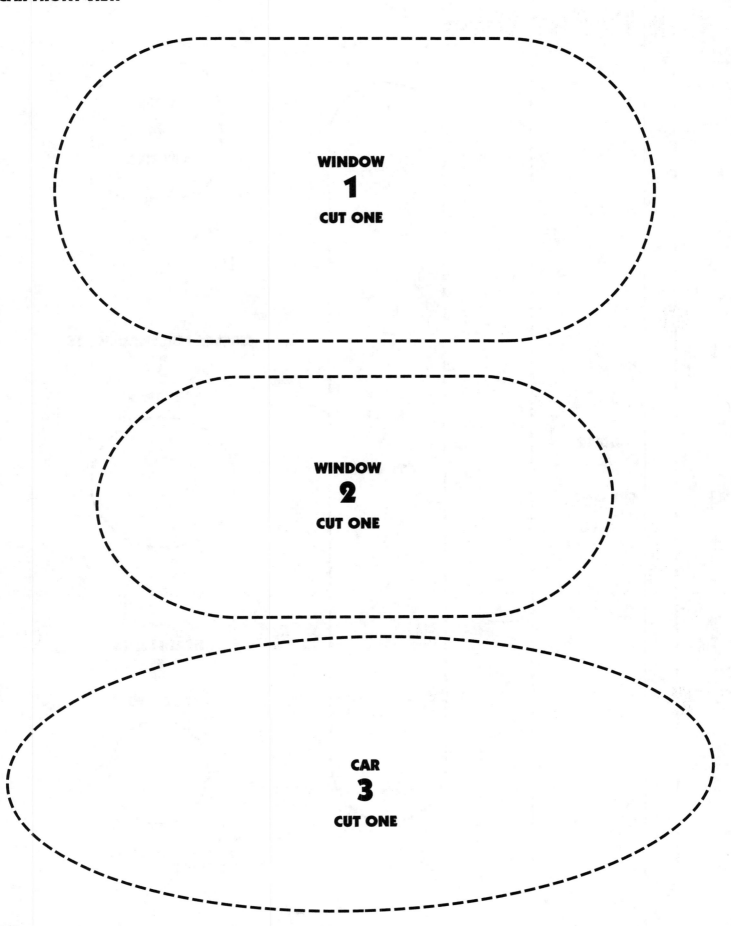

**WINDOW**
**1**
**CUT ONE**

**WINDOW**
**2**
**CUT ONE**

**CAR**
**3**
**CUT ONE**

# CAR FRONT VIEW

**BUMPER**
**4**
CUT ONE

**GRILL**
**5**
CUT ONE

**TIRES**
**6**
CUT TWO

**CIRCLES FOR HEADLIGHTS**
**7**
CUT TWO

**HEADLIGHTS**
**8**
CUT TWO

**Note:**
You can cut #8 headlights from foil
or silver-colored gift wrap.

# COMBINE

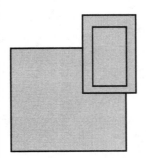
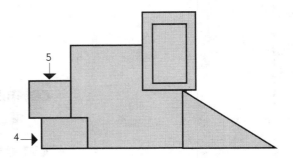

**1** Cut one #1 combine and one #2 cab from red paper and glue as shown.

**2** Cut one #3 cab door from red paper and glue to the cab.

**3** Cut one #4 back and one #5 back from red paper. Glue these to the back of the combine. Cut one #6 front from red paper and glue to the front of the combine.

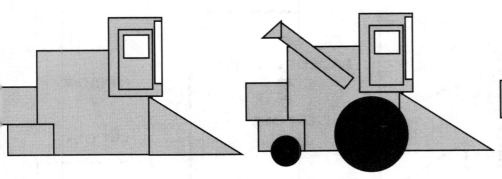

**4** Cut one #7 window and one #8 windows from white paper and glue as shown.

**5** Cut one #9 tube and one #10 spout from red paper and glue on the combine for the spout. Cut one #11 big wheel and one #12 small wheel from black paper. Glue the larger wheel to the front of the combine and the smaller one to the back.

**6** Cut one #13 big wheel and #one 14 small wheel from white paper. Glue the larger circle in the center of the big wheel. Glue the smaller circle in the center of the small wheel. Cut one #15 paddle from brown paper and glue behind the front of the combine.

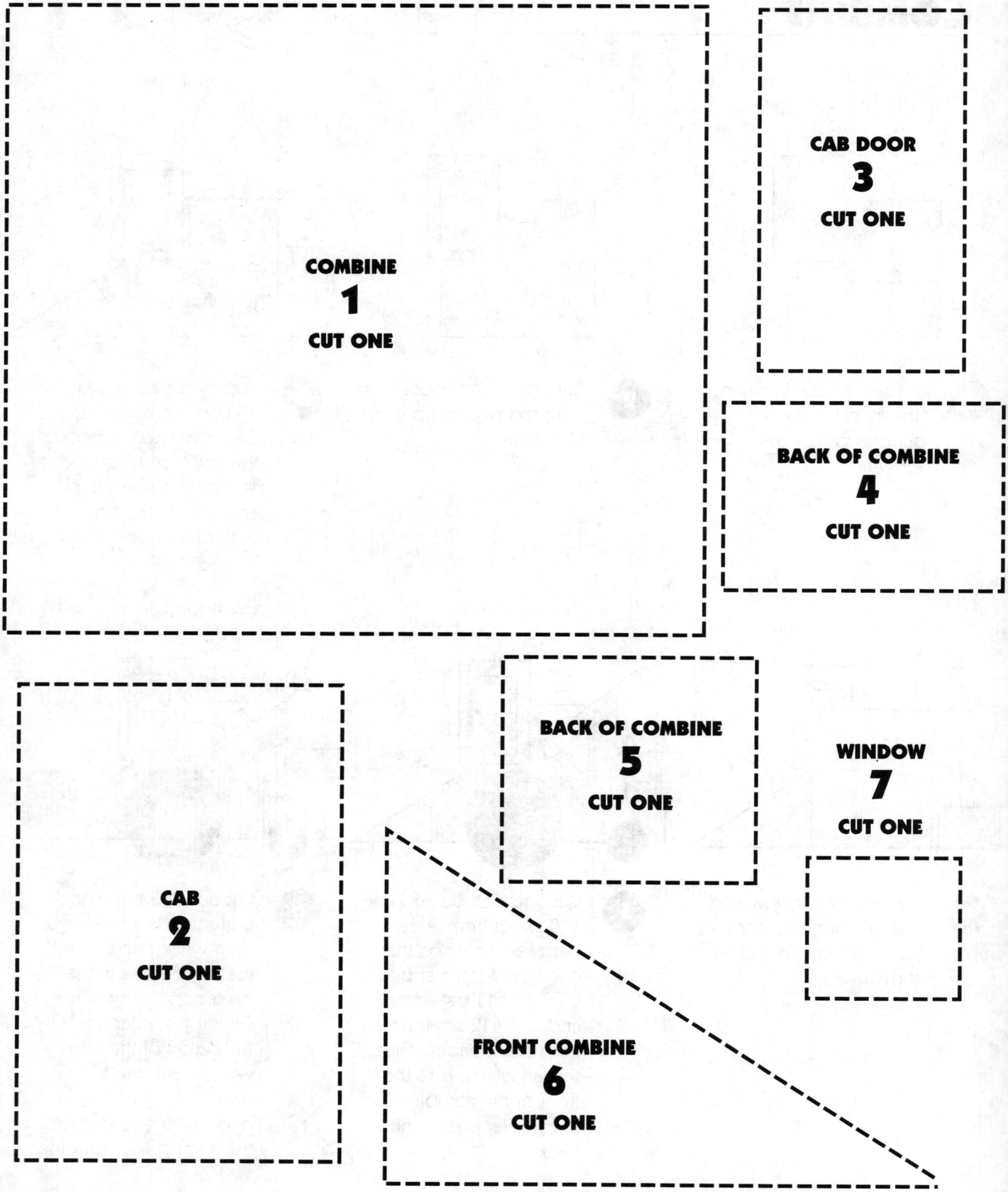

COMBINE
**1**
CUT ONE

CAB DOOR
**3**
CUT ONE

BACK OF COMBINE
**4**
CUT ONE

BACK OF COMBINE
**5**
CUT ONE

WINDOW
**7**
CUT ONE

CAB
**2**
CUT ONE

FRONT COMBINE
**6**
CUT ONE

# COMBINE PATTERNS

WINDOW
## 8
**CUT ONE**

TUBE
## 9
**CUT ONE**

BIG WHEEL
## 11
**CUT ONE**

SPOUT
## 10
**CUT ONE**

SMALL WHEEL
## 12
**CUT ONE**

BIG WHEEL
## 13
**CUT ONE**

SMALL WHEEL
## 14
**CUT ONE**

PADDLE
## 15
**CUT ONE**

# CRANE

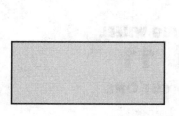

**1** Cut one #1 body from yellow paper.

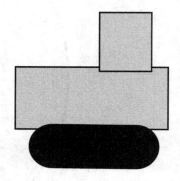

**2** Cut one #2 track from black paper and glue to the bottom of the body. Cut one #3 cab from yellow paper and glue to the top of the body as shown.

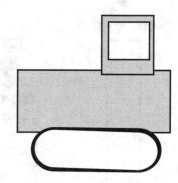

**3** Cut one #4 track from white paper and glue in the middle of the black track. Cut one #5 window from white paper and glue onto the cab.

**4** Cut two #6 wheels from gray paper and glue on each end of the white part of the tracks. Cut one #7 crane arm from yellow paper and glue as shown.

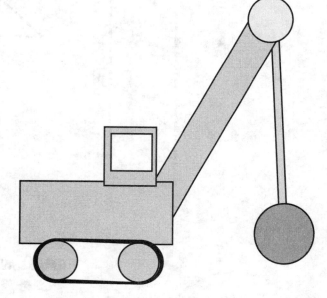

**5** Cut one #8 cable from gray paper and glue to the top of the crane arm. (Note: You can use string or yarn for this.) Cut one #9 wrecking ball from black or gray paper paper and glue to the bottom of the cable. Cut one #10 pulley from yellow paper and glue to the top of the crane arm as shown.

# CRANE PATTERNS

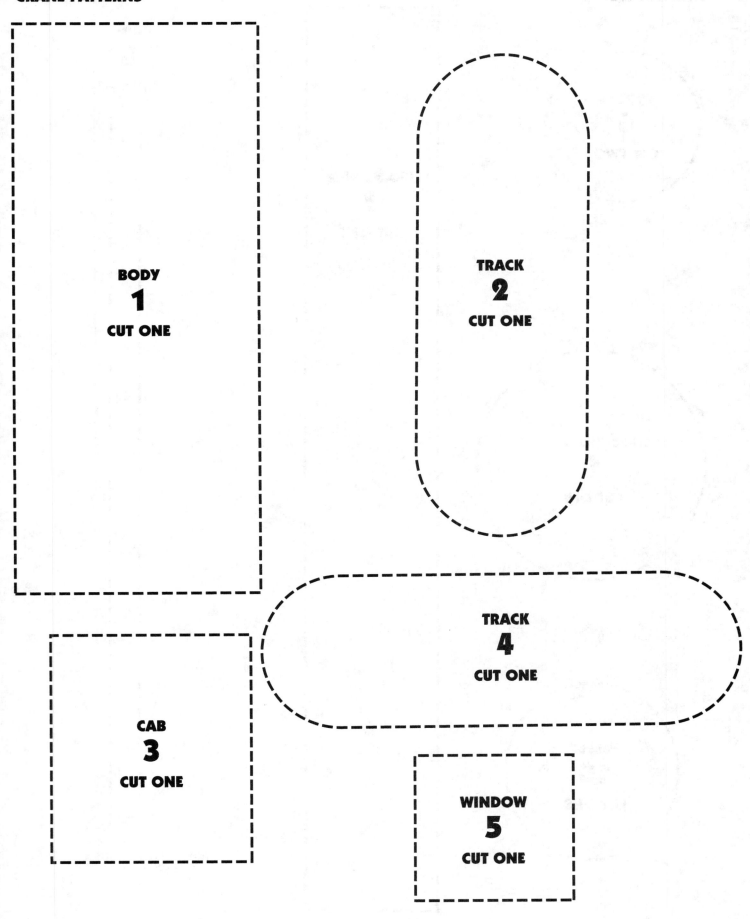

**BODY**
**1**
CUT ONE

**TRACK**
**2**
CUT ONE

**CAB**
**3**
CUT ONE

**TRACK**
**4**
CUT ONE

**WINDOW**
**5**
CUT ONE

# CRANE PATTERNS

WHEELS
**6**
CUT TWO

WRECKING BALL
**9**
CUT ONE

PULLEY
**10**
CUT ONE

CRANE ARM
**7**
CUT ONE

CABLE
**8**
CUT ONE

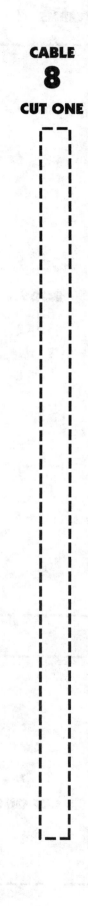

**Materials:** *black, red and white paper; scissors; glue; black crayon or marker*

# DUMP TRUCK

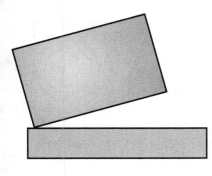 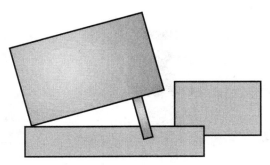 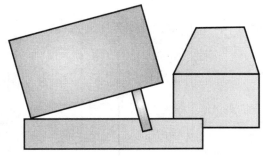

**1** Cut one #1 base and one #2 body from red paper.

**2** Cut one #3 lifter and one #4 hood from red paper and assemble as shown.

**3** Cut one #5 cab and glue on top of the hood.

**4** Cut two #6 wheels from black paper and two #7 hubcaps from white paper and glue one of each together to form two tires. Glue in place. Cut one #8 tailgate from red paper and glue to the back of the dump truck as shown.

**5** Cut one #9 window and two #10 windows from white paper and glue as shown. Cut one #11 bumper from white or gray paper and glue to the front of the dump truck.

# DUMP TRUCK PATTERNS

**LIFTER**
**3**
CUT ONE

**BODY**
**2**
CUT ONE

**BASE**
**1**
CUT ONE

**HOOD**
**4**
CUT ONE

# DUMP TRUCK PATTERNS

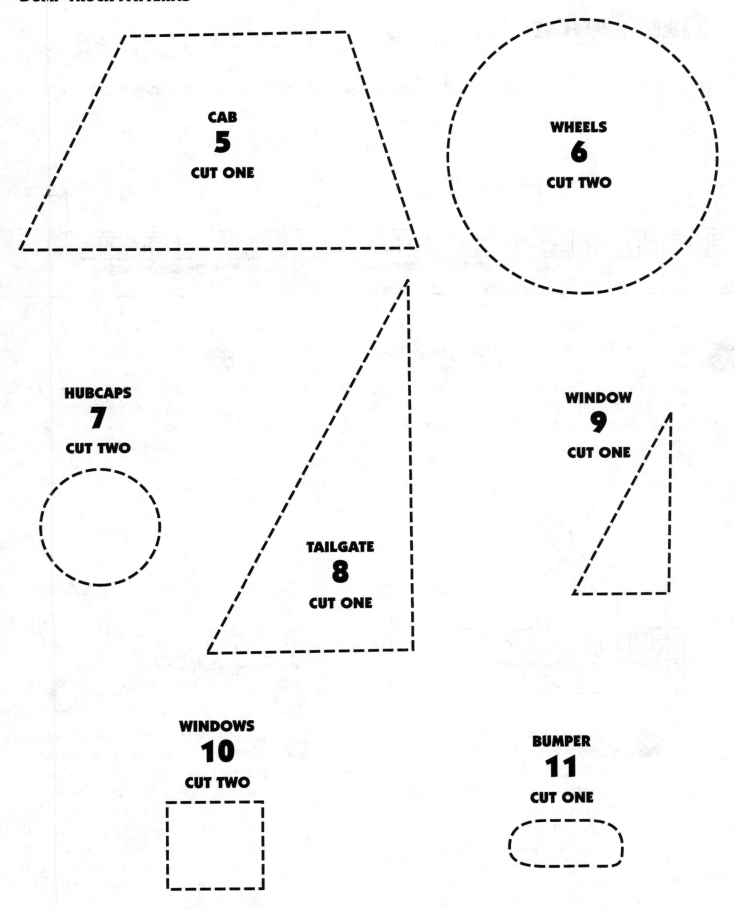

CAB
**5**
CUT ONE

WHEELS
**6**
CUT TWO

HUBCAPS
**7**
CUT TWO

TAILGATE
**8**
CUT ONE

WINDOW
**9**
CUT ONE

WINDOWS
**10**
CUT TWO

BUMPER
**11**
CUT ONE

**Materials:** *black, gray, red, white and yellow paper; scissors; glue; black crayon or marker*

# FIRE TRUCK

**Note:** You may want to draw on the ladder, control box and hose if you feel the pieces are too many or too small.

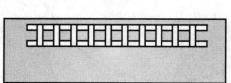  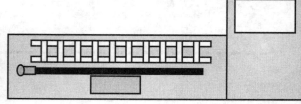

**1** Cut one #1 body from red paper. Cut two #2 ladder sides and ten #3 ladder rungs from white paper. Glue the ladder on first.

**2** For the hose, cut one #4 hose from black or white paper. Cut one #5 nozzle from yellow or gray paper and glue to the end of the hose as shown. Cut one #6 control box from gray paper and glue under the hose.

**3** Cut one #7 cab from red paper; glue to the front of the truck. Cut one #8 window from white paper and glue to the top of the cab.

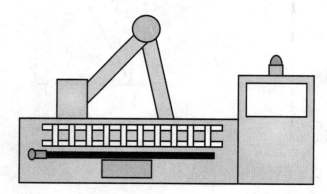 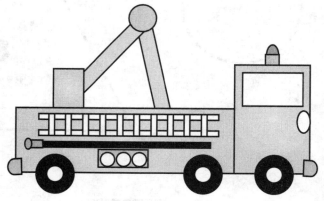

**4** Cut two #9 boom lifts from red paper and one #10 lift bucket from red paper and glue as shown. Cut one #11 pulley from red paper and glue on the two #9 pieces as shown. Cut one #12 siren base from gray paper and one #13 siren light from red paper. Glue the siren base and light on top of the cab as shown.

**5** Cut three #14 wheels from black paper and three #15 hubcaps from white paper to make three wheels. Glue in place as shown. Cut one #16 headlight from white paper and glue on front of the cab. Cut two #17 bumpers from gray paper and glue one to each end of the fire truck. Cut three #18 gauges from white paper and glue to the control box as shown.

# FIRE TRUCK PATTERNS

**LADDER SIDES**
**2**
**CUT TWO**

**HOSE**
**4**
**CUT ONE**

**LADDER RUNGS**
**3**
**CUT TEN**

**BODY**
**1**
**CUT ONE**

**NOZZLE**
**5**
**CUT ONE**

**CONTROL BOX**
**6**
**CUT ONE**

TLC10084 Copyright © Teaching & Learning Company, Carthage, IL 62321-0010

**CAB**
**7**
**CUT ONE**

**WINDOW**
**8**
**CUT ONE**

**LIFT BUCKET**
**10**
**CUT ONE**

**BOOM LIFTS**
**9**
**CUT TWO**

**PULLEY**
**11**
**CUT ONE**

**SIREN BASE**
**12**
**CUT ONE**

**SIREN LIGHT**
**13**
**CUT ONE**

**WHEELS**
**14**
**CUT THREE**

**HUBCAPS**
**15**
**CUT THREE**

**HEADLIGHT**
**16**
**CUT ONE**

**BUMPERS**
**17**
**CUT TWO**

**GAUGES**
**18**
**CUT THREE**

**Materials:** *black, blue and white paper; scissors; glue; black crayon or marker*

# GAS TRUCK

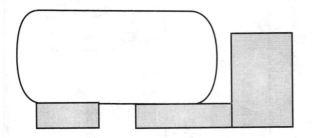

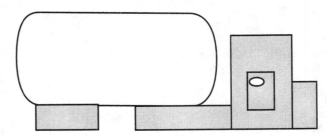

**1** Cut one #1 tank from white paper. Cut one #2 long truck base, one #3 short truck base and one #4 cab from blue paper. Glue #3 to the back of the tank. Glue #2 to the front of the tank, and glue the cab to #2.

**2** Cut one #5 engine and one #6 door from blue paper. Glue #5 to the front of the truck and #6 to the cab. Cut one #7 door handle from white or gray paper and glue as shown.

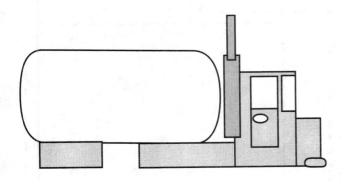

Gas Truck

**3** Cut one #8 window and one #9 windows and glue as shown. Cut one #10 muffler and one #11 exhaust from gray or black paper and glue as shown.

**4** Cut four #12 wheels from black paper and four #13 hubcaps from white paper to make three wheels. Glue in place. Cut one #14 bumper from gray paper and glue to the front of the truck. Cut one #15 headlight from white paper and glue on the front of the truck as shown. With a marker write *Gas Truck* on the side of the tank.

# Gas Truck

**Note:**
Copy or use these letters to trace onto the truck.

**LONG TRUCK BASE**
**2**
**CUT ONE**

**SHORT TRUCK BASE**
**3**
**CUT ONE**

**TANK**
**1**
**CUT ONE**

**CAB**
**4**
**CUT ONE**

# GAS TRUCK PATTERNS

**ENGINE**
**5**
CUT ONE

**DOOR**
**6**
CUT ONE

**DOOR HANDLE**
**7**
CUT ONE

**Note:**
Draw with marker or crayon if this piece is too small for your students to cut.

**WINDOW**
**8**
CUT ONE

**MUFFLER**
**10**
CUT ONE

**WINDOW**
**9**
CUT ONE

**EXHAUST**
**11**
CUT ONE

**WHEELS**
**12**
CUT FOUR

**HUBCAPS**
**13**
CUT FOUR

**BUMPER**
**14**
CUT ONE

**HEADLIGHT**
**15**
CUT ONE

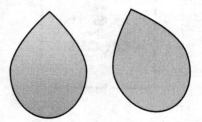

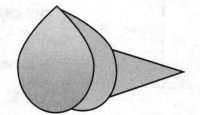

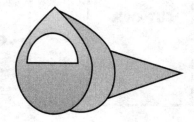

**1** Cut two #1 cabin pieces from light blue paper.

**2** Cut one #2 tail from light blue paper. Assemble the pieces as shown and glue.

**3** Cut one #3 window from white paper and glue to the front of the helicopter.

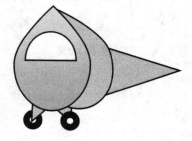

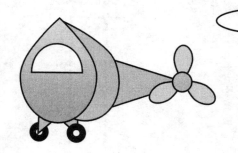

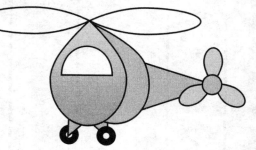

**4** Cut two #4 legs from light blue paper. Glue one to each side of the helicopter. Cut two #5 wheels from black paper and two #6 hubcaps from white paper. Glue one of each together and glue to the legs as shown.

**5** Cut three #7 tail rotor blades from gray or white paper. Cut one #8 circle for propeller from light blue paper and glue to the center of the tail rotor blades as shown.

**6** Cut two #9 rotor blades from white paper and glue to the top of the helicopter.

# HELICOPTER PATTERNS

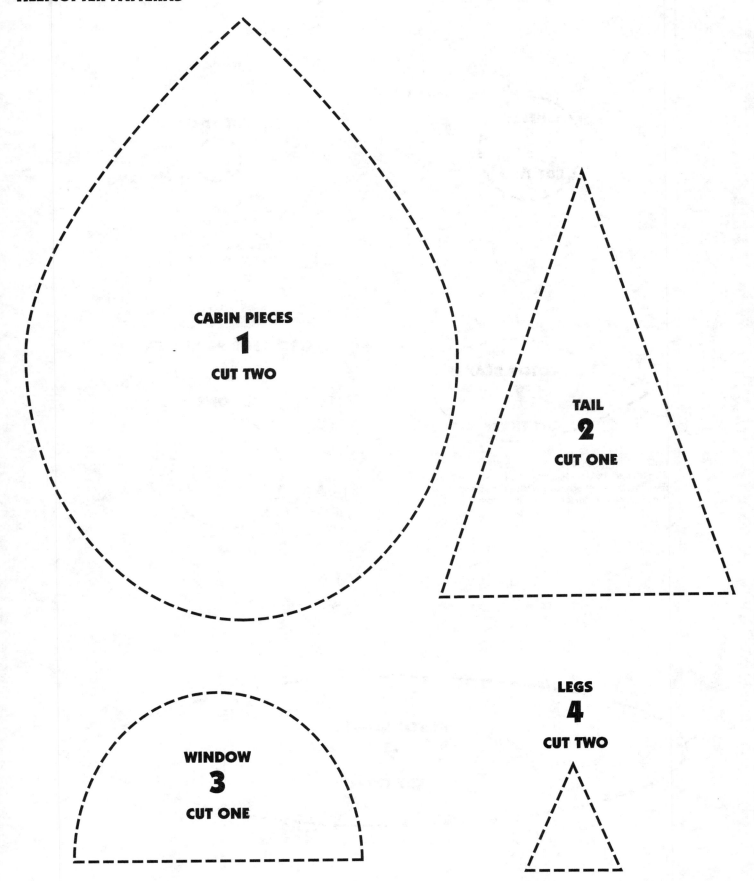

CABIN PIECES
**1**
CUT TWO

TAIL
**2**
CUT ONE

WINDOW
**3**
CUT ONE

LEGS
**4**
CUT TWO

**WHEELS**
**5**
**CUT TWO**

**HUBCAPS**
**6**
**CUT TWO**

**Note:**
Draw hubcaps on with marker or crayon if this piece is too small for your students to cut or use a round white sticker.

**TAIL ROTOR BLADES**
**7**
**CUT THREE**

**Note:**
Glue tail rotor blades together with points overlapping. Let dry completely. Attach to tail with a brad fastener. Make sure there is enough room for the blades to spin.

**CIRCLE FOR PROPELLER**
**8**
**CUT ONE**

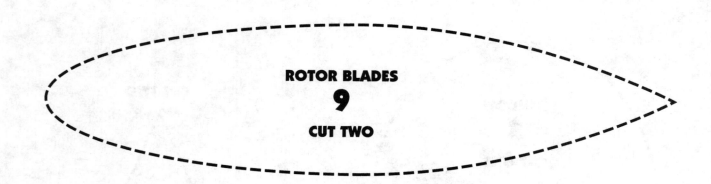

**ROTOR BLADES**
**9**
**CUT TWO**

**Materials:** black, golden yellow and white paper; scissors; glue; black crayon or marker

# LOADER

 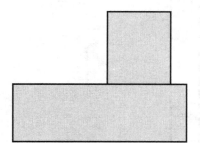 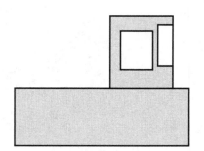

**1** Cut one #1 body from golden yellow paper.

**2** Cut one #2 cab from golden yellow paper and glue to body as shown.

**3** Cut one #3 and one #4 window from white paper and glue as shown.

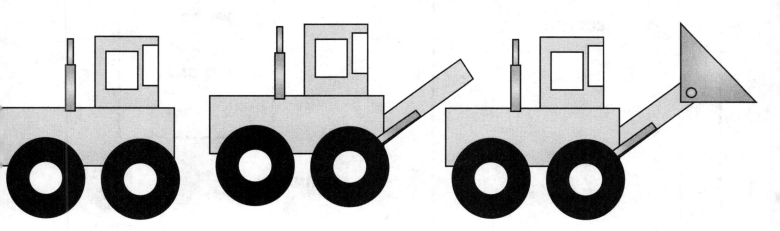

**4** Cut one #5 muffler and one #6 exhaust from gray or black paper. Glue as shown. Cut two #7 wheels from black paper and two #8 hubcaps from white paper and glue in place.

**5** Cut one #9 lifter arm from golden yellow paper and one #10 strut from gray paper. Glue #9 toward the back of the loader, and glue the strut on the front side of the #9 lifter arm.

**6** Cut one #11 bucket from golden yellow paper and glue to the end of the lifter arm. Cut one #12 circle for the bucket from gray paper or use a marker to make a circle for the bucket and glue in place as shown.

# LOADER PATTERNS

**CAB**
**2**
**CUT ONE**

**BODY**
**1**
**CUT ONE**

**WINDOW**
**3**
**CUT ONE**

**WINDOW**
**4**
**CUT ONE**

**MUFFLER**
**5**
**CUT ONE**

# LOADER PATTERNS

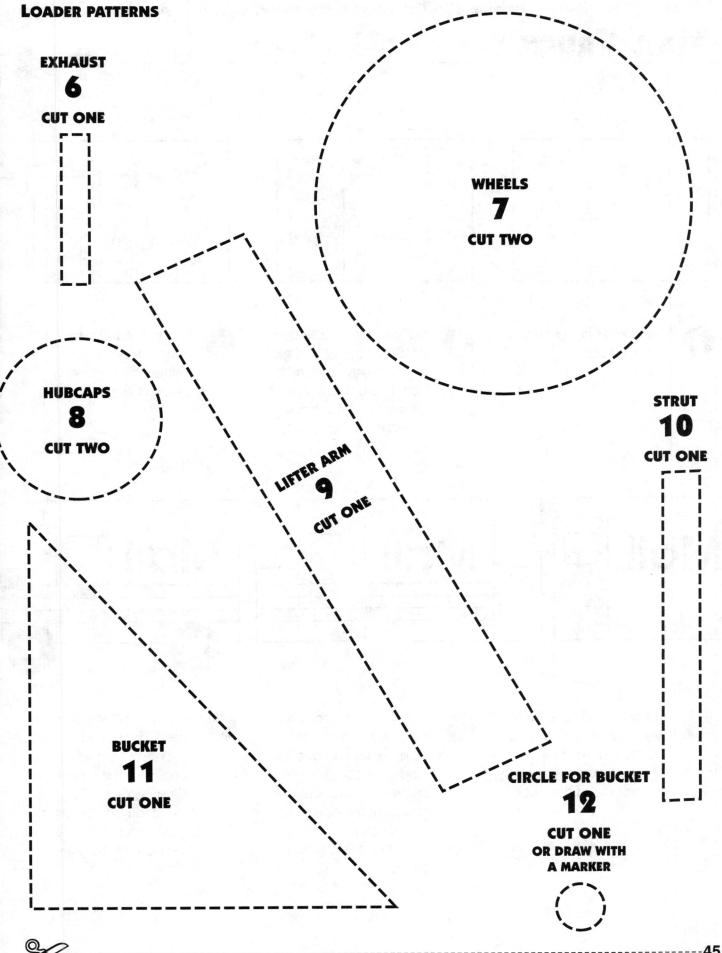

**EXHAUST**
**6**
CUT ONE

**WHEELS**
**7**
CUT TWO

**HUBCAPS**
**8**
CUT TWO

**STRUT**
**10**
CUT ONE

**LIFTER ARM**
**9**
CUT ONE

**BUCKET**
**11**
CUT ONE

**CIRCLE FOR BUCKET**
**12**
CUT ONE
OR DRAW WITH
A MARKER

**Materials:** black, blue, light gray, red and white paper; scissors; glue; black crayon or marker

# MAIL TRUCK

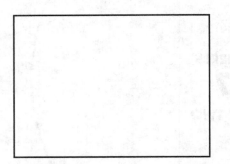 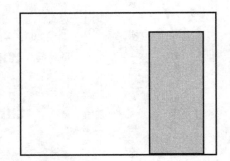 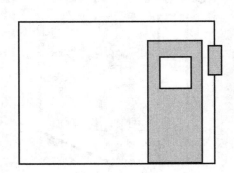

**1** Cut one #1 body from white paper.

**2** Cut one #2 door from light gray paper and glue on the body. (Note: If you glue down only one long side of the door, it will open and close.)

**3** Cut one #3 window from white paper. Cut one #4 mirror from light gray paper. Glue as shown.

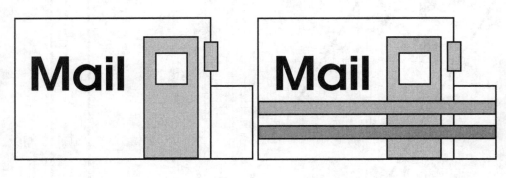 

**4** Cut one #5 engine from white paper and glue to the front of the truck. With a marker, write *Mail* on the side of the truck.

**5** Cut two #6 stripes one from red and one from blue paper. Glue to the side of the truck as shown. (Note: Cut the stripes at the open side of the door if you've only glued one side in step 2.)

**6** Cut two #7 wheels from black paper and two #8 hubcaps from white paper for the wheels. Glue in place. Cut one #9 headlight from light gray paper and glue to the front of the mail truck.

**BODY**
**1**
**CUT ONE**

# MAIL TRUCK PATTERNS

**STRIPES**
**6**
CUT TWO

**WINDOW**
**3**
CUT ONE

**DOOR**
**2**
CUT ONE

**ENGINE**
**5**
CUT ONE

**MIRROR**
**4**
CUT ONE

**WHEELS**
**7**
CUT TWO

**HUBCAPS**
**8**
CUT TWO

**HEADLIGHT**
**9**
CUT ONE

# Mail

**Note:**
Copy or use these letters to trace onto the truck.

**Materials:** *black, gray and white paper; scissors; glue; black crayon or marker*

# MILK TRUCK

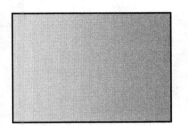

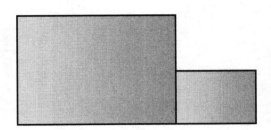

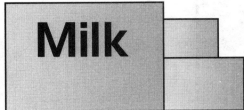

**1** Cut one #1 body from gray paper.

**2** Cut one #2 engine from gray paper and glue to the front of the truck.

**3** Cut one #3 cab from gray paper and glue to the top of the engine.

**4** Cut one #4 window from white paper and glue in the middle of the cab as shown. With a marker, write *Milk* on the side of the truck.

**5** Cut one #5 bumper from gray or white paper and glue to the front of the truck.

**6** Cut two #6 wheels from black paper and two #7 hubcaps from white paper. Glue the hubcaps in the center of the wheels and then glue to the truck as shown.

**BODY**
**1**
**CUT ONE**

# MILK TRUCK PATTERNS

ENGINE
## 2
CUT ONE

WINDOW
## 4
CUT ONE

BUMPER
## 5
CUT TWO

CAB
## 3
CUT ONE

WHEELS
## 6
CUT TWO

HUBCAPS
## 7
CUT ONE

**Note:**
Copy or use these letters to trace onto the truck.

TLC10084 Copyright © Teaching & Learning Company, Carthage, IL  62321-0010

**Materials:** black, blue, gray and white paper; scissors; glue; black crayon or marker

# MIXER TRUCK

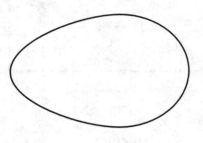
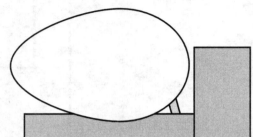
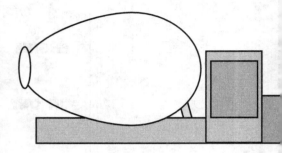

**1** Cut one #1 mixer from white paper.

**2** Cut one #2 base and one #3 cab from blue paper. Glue the base to the back at the bottom of the mixer. Glue the cab to the base. Cut one #4 lift from gray paper and glue to the back of the mixer and base.

**3** Cut one #5 door from blue paper. Cut one #6 engine from blue paper and glue as shown. Cut one #7 hatch from white paper and glue to the back of the mixer.

**4** Cut one #8 window from white paper and glue to the door. Cut one #9 canopy for the cab from blue paper and glue to the back at the top of the cab. Cut one #10 gas tank from gray paper and glue to the base.

**5** Cut three #11 wheels from black paper and three #12 hubcaps from white paper. Glue the hubcaps in the center of the wheels and then glue tot he truck. Cut one #13 headlight from white paper and glue to the front as shown. Cut one #14 bumper from gray paper and glue to the front of the truck.

# MIXER TRUCK PATTERNS

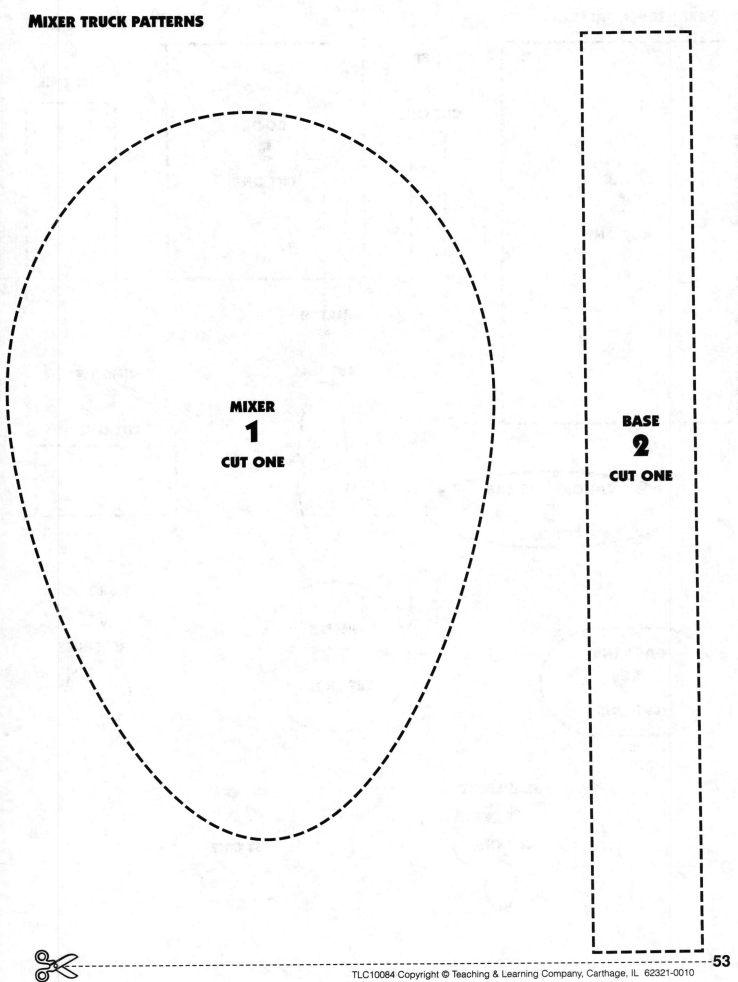

MIXER
**1**
CUT ONE

BASE
**2**
CUT ONE

# MIXER TRUCK PATTERNS

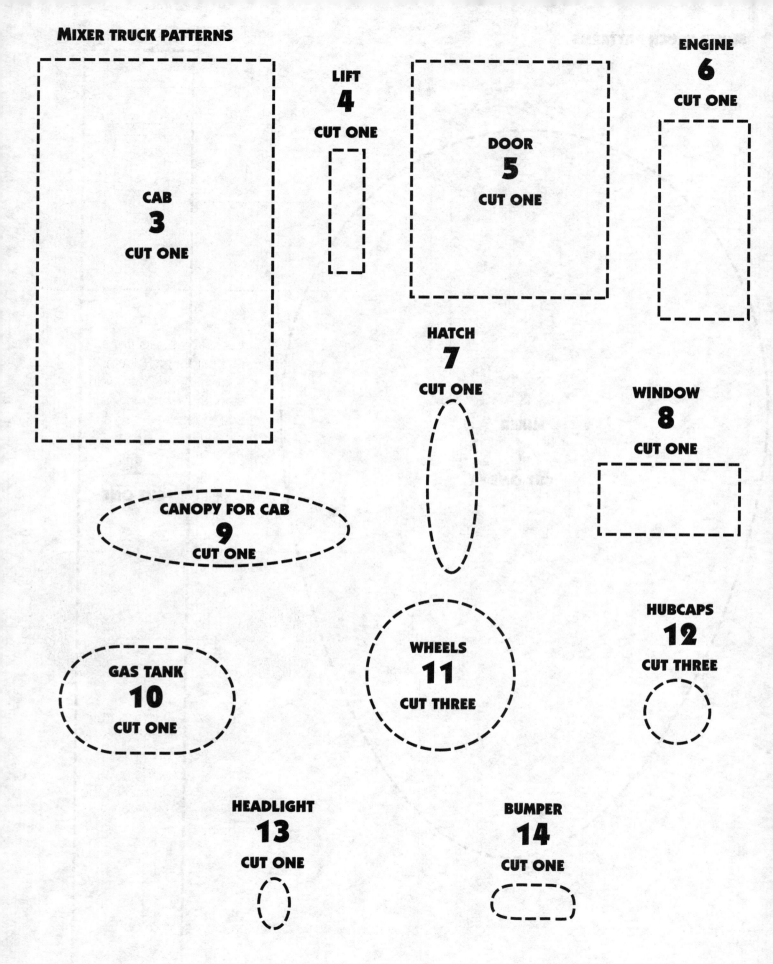

CAB
**3**
CUT ONE

LIFT
**4**
CUT ONE

DOOR
**5**
CUT ONE

ENGINE
**6**
CUT ONE

HATCH
**7**
CUT ONE

WINDOW
**8**
CUT ONE

CANOPY FOR CAB
**9**
CUT ONE

GAS TANK
**10**
CUT ONE

WHEELS
**11**
CUT THREE

HUBCAPS
**12**
CUT THREE

HEADLIGHT
**13**
CUT ONE

BUMPER
**14**
CUT ONE

**Materials:** black, gray, red and white paper; scissors; glue; black crayon or marker

# PICKUP TRUCK

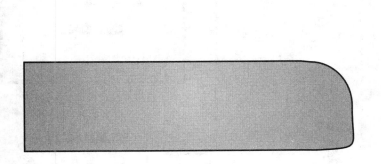

**1** Cut one #1 body from red paper.

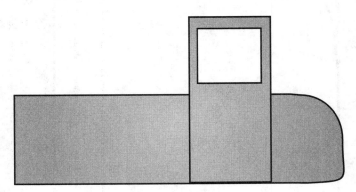

**2** Cut one # 2 cab from red paper and glue as shown. Cut one #3 window from white paper and glue to the cab as shown.

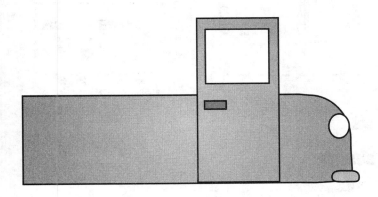

**3** Cut one #4 headlight from white paper and glue to the front of the body. Cut one #5 door handle from gray paper and glue to the cab. Cut one #6 bumper from gray paper and glue to the front of the truck as shown.

**4** Cut two #7 wheels from black paper and two #8 hubcaps from white paper. Glue the hubcaps in the center of the wheels and then glue to the truck.

**Note:** Draw or cut out pictures from magazines of various things to put in the back of your truck.

# PICKUP TRUCK PATTERNS

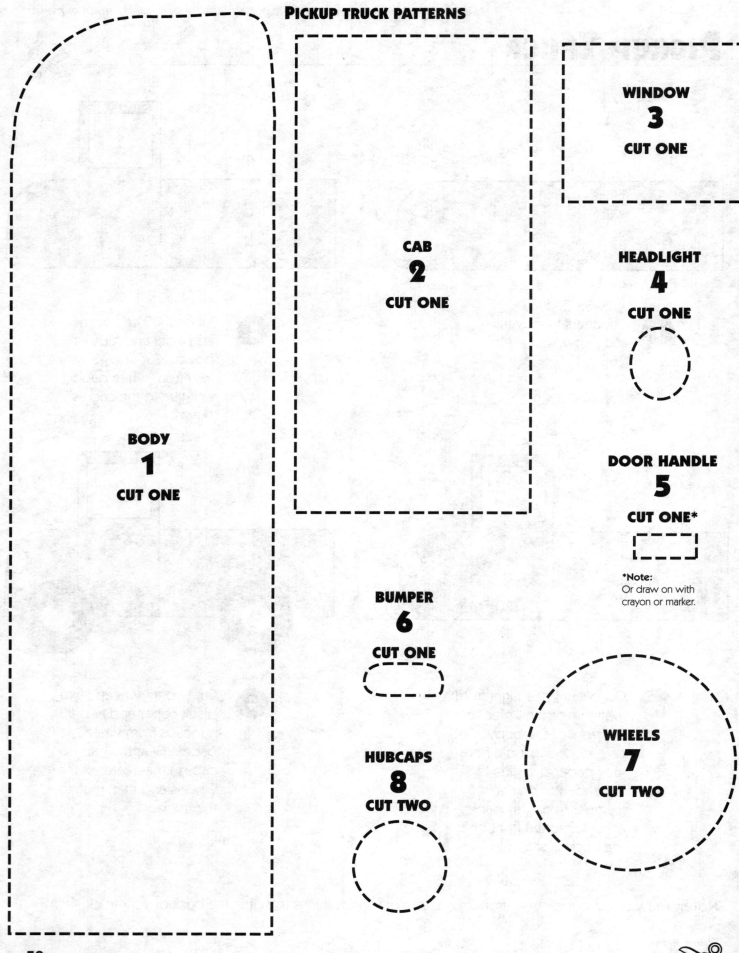

**WINDOW**
**3**
CUT ONE

**CAB**
**2**
CUT ONE

**HEADLIGHT**
**4**
CUT ONE

**BODY**
**1**
CUT ONE

**DOOR HANDLE**
**5**
CUT ONE*

*Note:
Or draw on with
crayon or marker.

**BUMPER**
**6**
CUT ONE

**WHEELS**
**7**
CUT TWO

**HUBCAPS**
**8**
CUT TWO

**Materials:** *blue, brown, red and white paper; scissors; glue; black crayon or marker*

# SAILBOAT

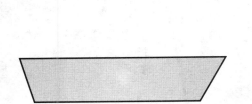

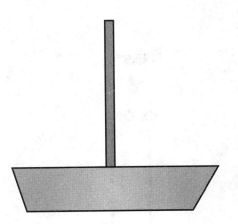

**1** Cut one #1 hull from blue paper.

**2** Cut one #2 mast from brown paper.

**3** Cut one #3 topsail from white paper and glue to the back of the mast.

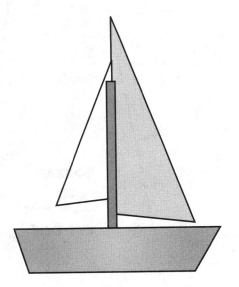

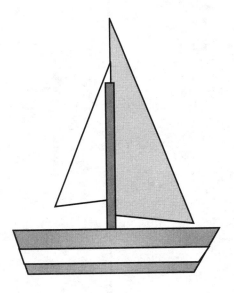

**4** Cut one #4 mainsail from blue paper and glue to the other side of the mast.

**5** Cut one #5 stripe from white paper and glue to the hull.

**Note:** These make an appealing bulletin board display. Have children make boats out of brightly colored paper (a wallpaper sample book would work well) and place on a background of royal blue. These also make attractive desk tags, cubby tags or coatrack labels, with children's names written on the hull.

# SAILBOAT PATTERNS

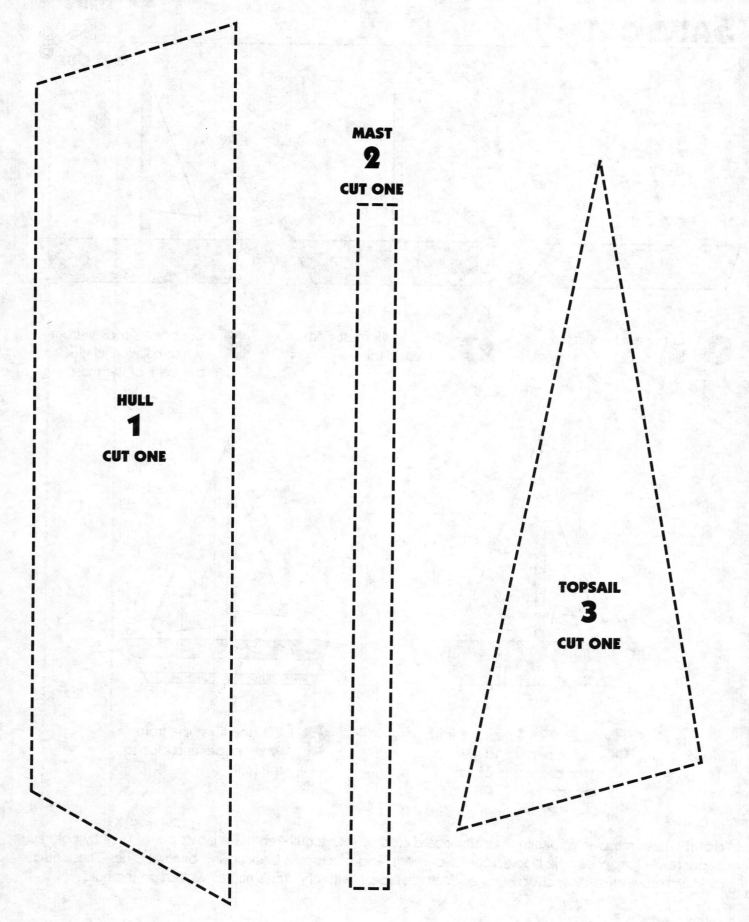

MAST

**2**

CUT ONE

HULL

**1**

CUT ONE

TOPSAIL

**3**

CUT ONE

# SAILBOAT PATTERNS

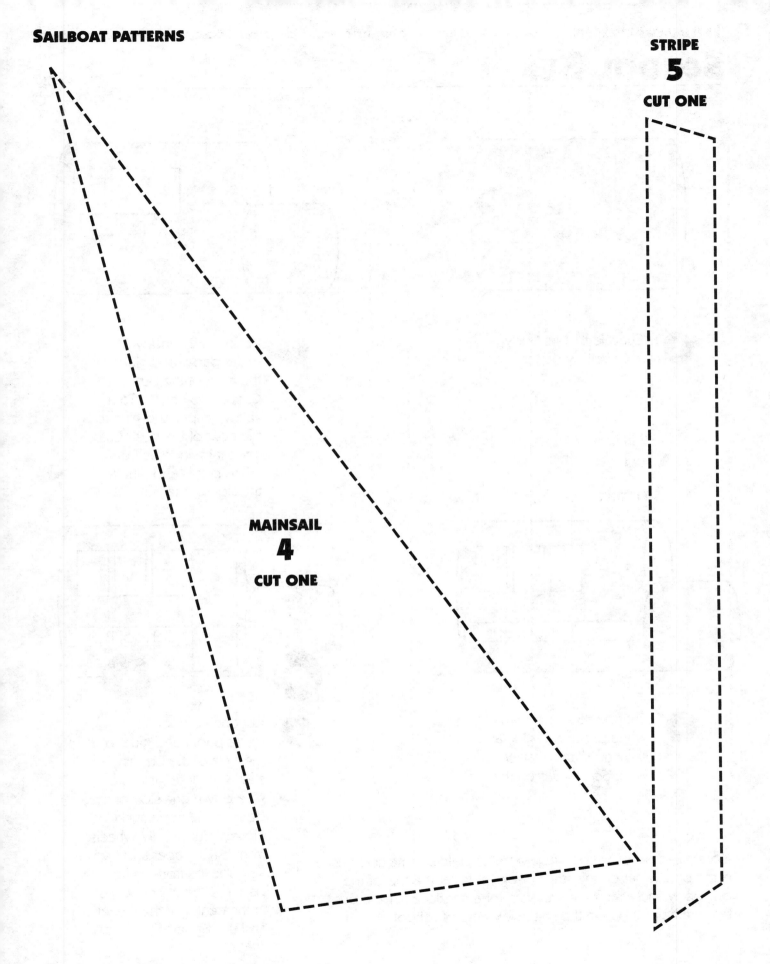

STRIPE
**5**
CUT ONE

MAINSAIL
**4**
CUT ONE

TLC10084 Copyright © Teaching & Learning Company, Carthage, IL 62321-0010 **59**

**Materials:** *black, white and yellow paper; scissors; glue; black crayon or marker*

# SCHOOL BUS

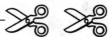

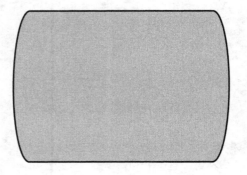

**1** Cut one #1 bus body from yellow paper.

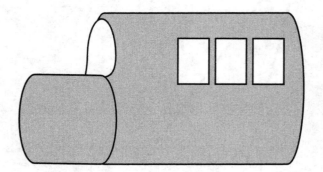

**2** Cut one #2 window from white paper and glue to the front of the bus. Cut one #3 engine from yellow paper and glue to the front of the bus. Cut three #4 windows from white paper and glue to the side of the bus.

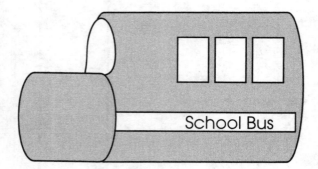

**3** Cut one #5 stripe from white paper and glue as shown. With a marker, write *School Bus* on the side.

**4** Cut one #6 door from white paper and glue to the side of the bus as shown. (Note: If you only glue down one side of the door, it will open and close.) Cut two #7 wheels from black paper and two #8 hubcaps from white paper. Glue the hubcaps in the center of the wheels and then glue to the bus.

**Note:** Instead of *School Bus*, write the child's name and bus name or number on the stripe. Poke holes at the top of the bus body and attach string or yarn for a necklace. These bus tags are helpful during the first few weeks of school.

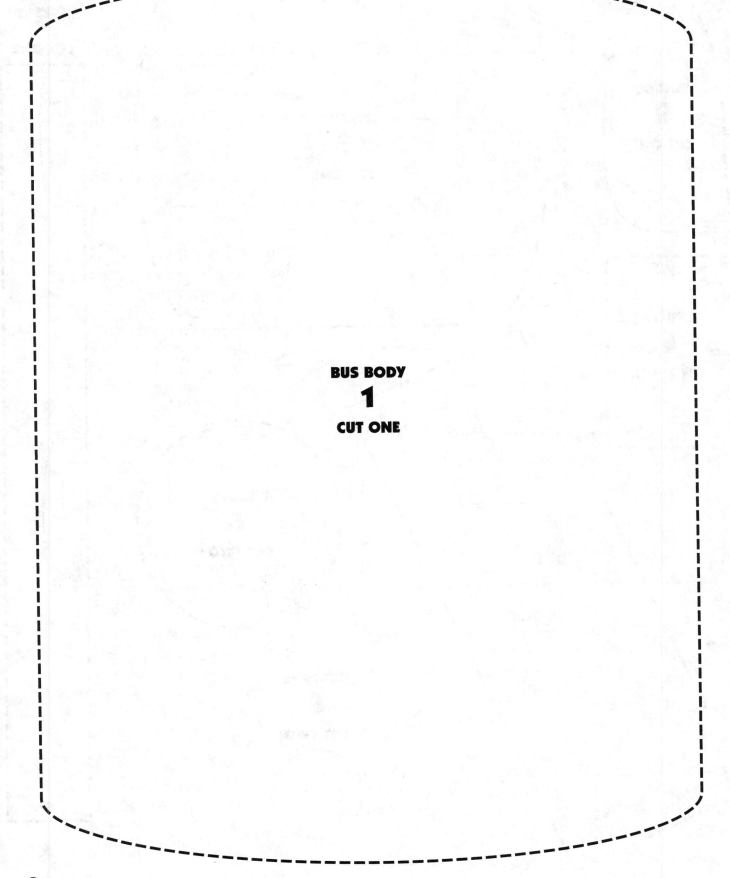

BUS BODY
**1**
CUT ONE

# SCHOOL BUS PATTERNS

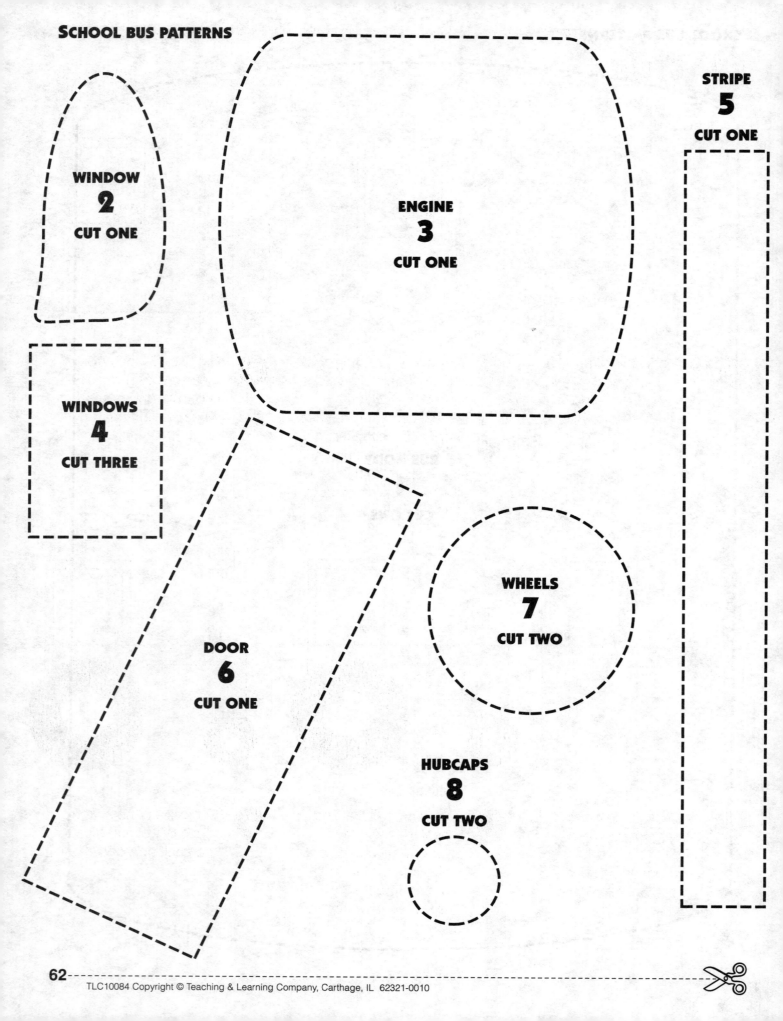

WINDOW
**2**
CUT ONE

ENGINE
**3**
CUT ONE

STRIPE
**5**
CUT ONE

WINDOWS
**4**
CUT THREE

DOOR
**6**
CUT ONE

WHEELS
**7**
CUT TWO

HUBCAPS
**8**
CUT TWO

**Materials:** *black, gray, two shades of green and white paper; scissors; glue; black crayon or marker*

# TRACTOR

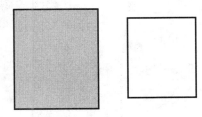 

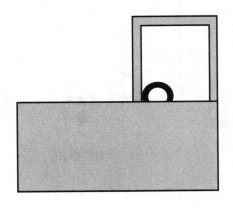

**1** Cut one #1 cab from green paper and one #2 cab window from white paper. These form the cab.

**2** Cut one #3 steering wheel from black paper and one #4 steering wheel center from white paper. Glue the #4 piece to the center of the #3 piece. Then glue to the bottom corner of the cab window.

**3** Cut one #5 body from green paper and glue to cab, over the steering wheel, as shown.

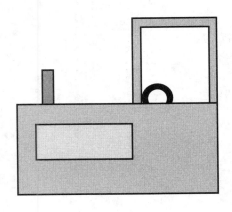

**4** Cut one #6 engine from gray or lighter green paper. Cut one #7 muffler from gray paper and glue to the top of the body as shown.

**5** Cut one #8 wheel and one #10 wheel from black paper and one #9 hubcap and one #11 hubcap from white paper. Glue wheels as shown.

**6** Cut one #12 hitch from green paper and glue to the back side of the big wheel.

CAB

**1**

CUT ONE

BODY

**5**

CUT ONE

CAB WINDOW

**2**

CUT ONE

# TRACTOR PATTERNS

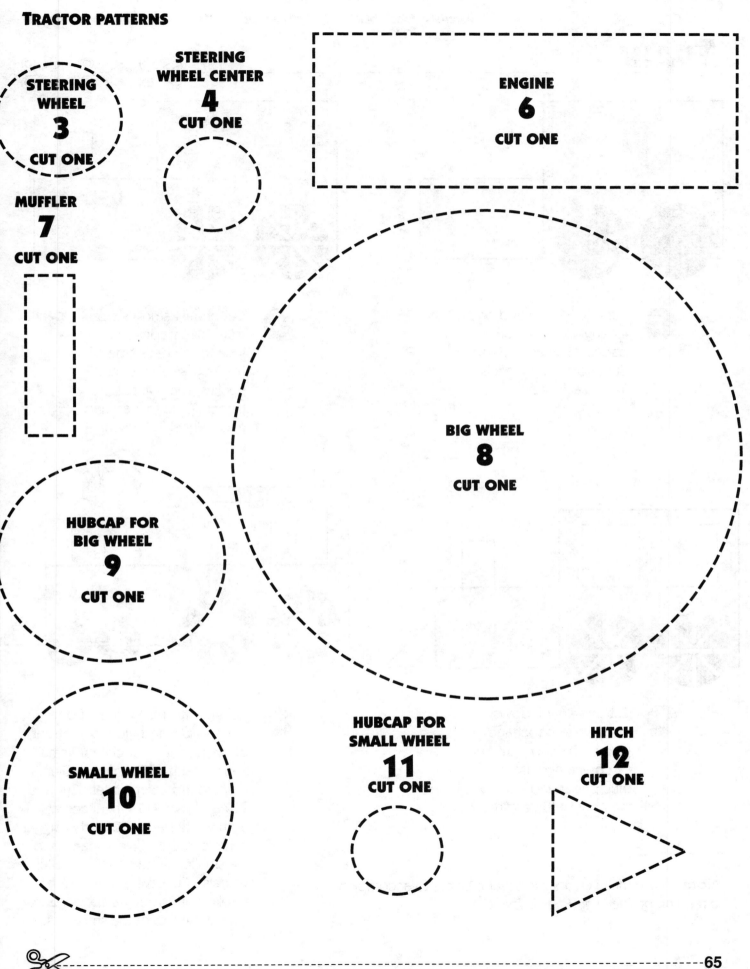

STEERING WHEEL
**3**
CUT ONE

STEERING WHEEL CENTER
**4**
CUT ONE

ENGINE
**6**
CUT ONE

MUFFLER
**7**
CUT ONE

BIG WHEEL
**8**
CUT ONE

HUBCAP FOR BIG WHEEL
**9**
CUT ONE

SMALL WHEEL
**10**
CUT ONE

HUBCAP FOR SMALL WHEEL
**11**
CUT ONE

HITCH
**12**
CUT ONE

# TRAIN

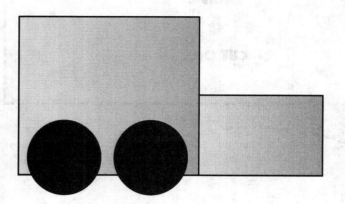

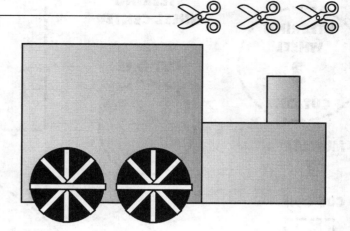

**1** Cut one #1 cab and one #2 engine from blue paper. Glue as shown. Cut two #3 big wheels from black paper.

**2** Cut one #4 smokestack from blue paper and glue to the back side of the engine. Cut eight #5 spokes from white paper. Glue four around each wheel as shown.

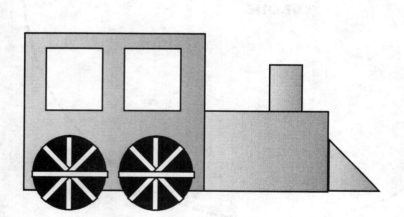

**3** Cut two #6 windows from white paper and glue to the cab. Cut one #7 cowcatcher from blue paper and glue to the front of the engine.

**4** Cut two #8 small wheels from black paper and glue to the front of the engine. Cut eight #9 small spokes from white paper. Glue four around each wheel. Cut two #10 and two #11 wheel centers from white paper. Glue the bigger centers to the bigger wheels and the smaller centers to the smaller wheels. Cut several different #12 smoke puffs from gray paper and glue at the top of the smokestack.

**Note:** Make these engines in several colors to accompany a reading of *The Little Engine That Could.*

**CAB**

**1**

**CUT ONE**

**ENGINE**

**2**

**CUT ONE**

# TRAIN PATTERNS

**BIG WHEELS**
**3**
CUT TWO

**SMOKESTACK**
**4**
CUT ONE

**SPOKES**
**5**
CUT EIGHT

**WINDOWS**
**6**
CUT TWO

**COWCATCHER**
**7**
CUT ONE

**SMALL WHEELS**
**8**
CUT TWO

**SMOKE PUFFS**
**12**
CUT SEVERAL

**SMALL SPOKES**
**9**
CUT EIGHT

**BIG WHEEL CENTERS**
**10**
CUT TWO

**SMALL WHEEL CENTERS**
**11**
CUT TWO

# TRAIN BOXCAR

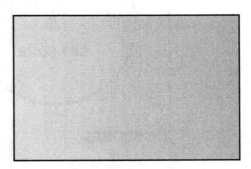

**1** Cut one #1 body from yellow paper.

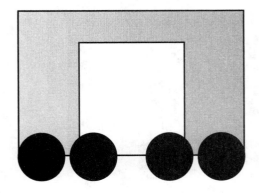

**2** Cut one #2 doors from white paper and glue to the body as shown. Cut four #3 wheels from black paper and glue as shown.

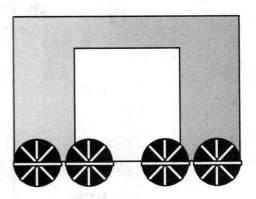

**3** Cut sixteen #4 spokes from white paper and glue four to each wheel as illustrated.

**4** Cut four #5 wheel centers from white paper and glue to the center of the wheels. Cut four #6 hinges from black paper and glue as shown. With a marker, draw a line down the middle of the doors. Cut two #7 knobs for the center of the door and glue as shown. (Note: You can use a marker to make the hinges and the knobs.)

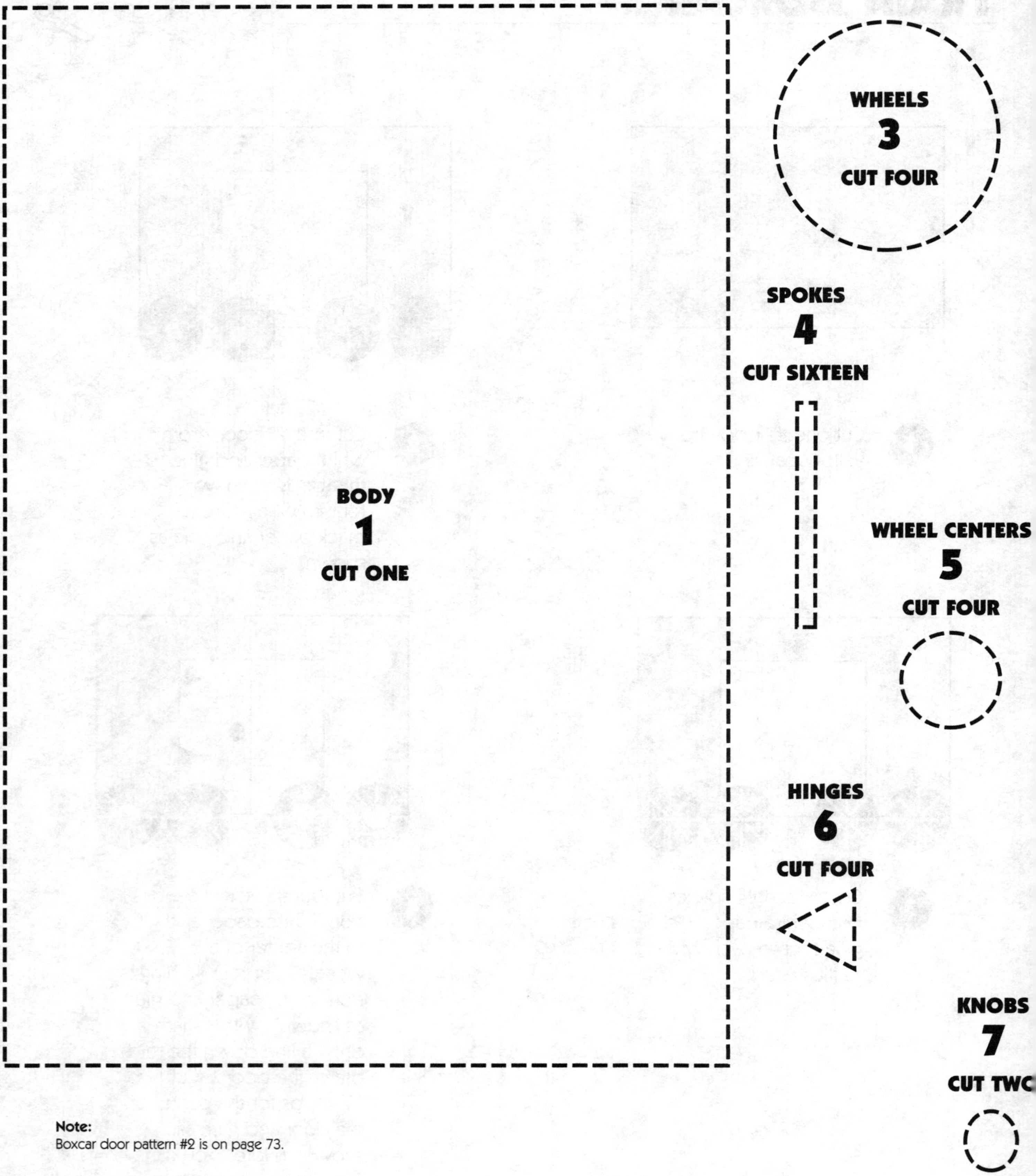

WHEELS
**3**
CUT FOUR

SPOKES
**4**
CUT SIXTEEN

BODY
**1**
CUT ONE

WHEEL CENTERS
**5**
CUT FOUR

HINGES
**6**
CUT FOUR

KNOBS
**7**
CUT TWO

Note:
Boxcar door pattern #2 is on page 73.

**Materials:** black, red and white paper; scissors; glue; black crayon or marker

# TRAIN CABOOSE

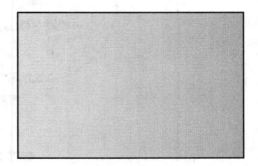

**1** Cut one #1 body from red paper.

**2** Cut four #2 wheels from black paper and glue as shown.

**3** Cut sixteen #3 spokes from white paper and glue four to each wheel. Cut four #4 wheel centers from white paper and glue to the center of the wheels. Cut two #5 windows from white paper and glue as shown. Cut one #6 crow's nest from red paper and glue to the top of the body.

**4** Cut three #7 windows from white paper and glue as shown. Cut one #8 top from gray or black paper and glue to the top of the crow's nest. Cut one #9 caboose end from red paper and glue to the end of the caboose.

# Train Caboose Patterns

WHEELS
## 2
CUT FOUR

SPOKES
## 3
CUT SIXTEEN

WHEEL CENTERS
## 4
CUT FOUR

BODY
## 1
CUT ONE

CROW'S NEST
## 6
CUT ONE

WINDOWS
## 7
CUT THREE

TOP FOR CROW'S NEST
## 8
CUT ONE

**DOORS FOR BOXCAR**
**2**
CUT ONE

**WINDOWS FOR CABOOSE**
**5**
CUT TWO

**CABOOSE END**
**9**
CUT ONE

**Materials:** *black, gray and white paper; scissors; glue; black crayon or marker*

# TRAIN FUEL TANK

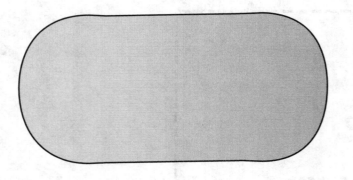

**1** Cut one #1 tank from gray or white paper.

**2** Cut four #2 wheels from black paper and glue as shown.

**3** Cut sixteen #3 spokes from white paper and glue four to each wheel. Cut one #4 stripe from white paper and glue to the center of the tank.

**4** Cut four #5 wheel centers from white paper and glue to the center of the wheels as shown. With a marker, write *Fuel* on the side of the stripe.

# Train fuel tank patterns

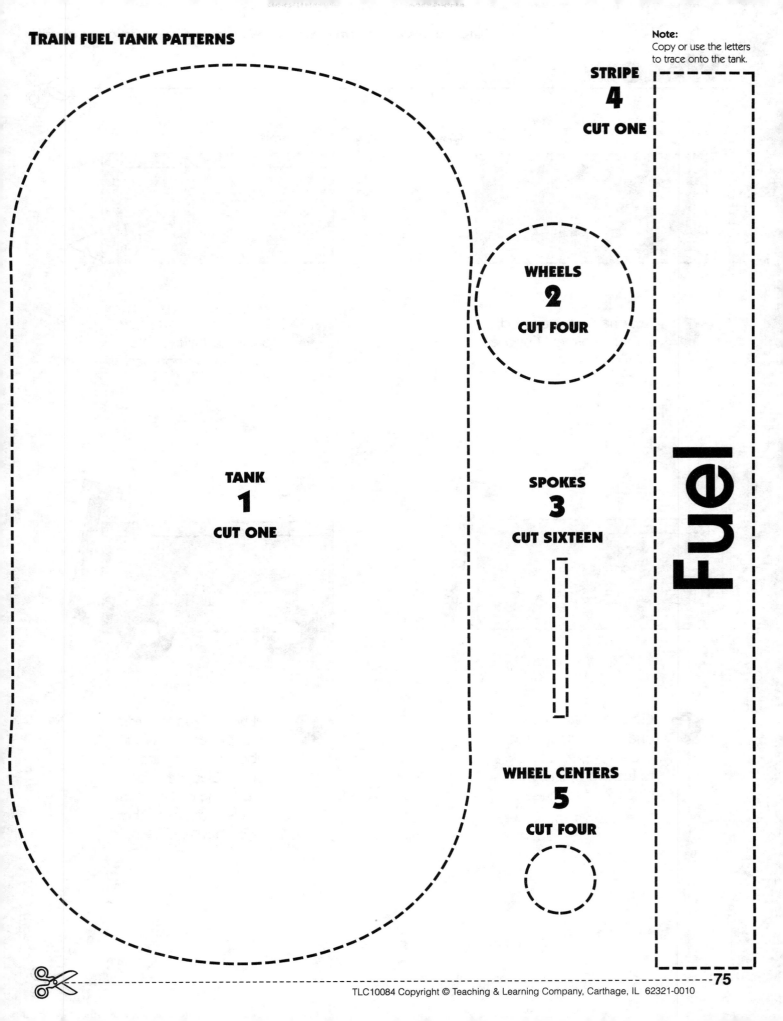

**Note:**
Copy or use the letters to trace onto the tank.

STRIPE
**4**
CUT ONE

WHEELS
**2**
CUT FOUR

TANK
**1**
CUT ONE

SPOKES
**3**
CUT SIXTEEN

Fuel

WHEEL CENTERS
**5**
CUT FOUR

# WAGON

**1** Cut one #1 wagon bed from red paper. Cut one #2 tongue from gray paper.

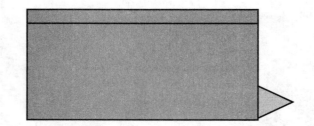

**2** Cut one #3 rim from red paper and glue at the top of the wagon bed as shown.

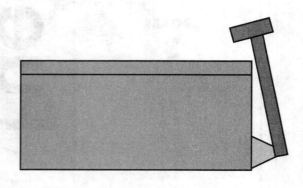

**3** Cut one #4 handle and one #5 handlebar from brown paper. Glue #5 to the top of #4. Then glue to the tongue as shown.

**4** Cut two #6 wheels from black paper and two #7 hubcaps from white paper. Glue the hubcaps to the center of the wheels and glue to the wagon bed as shown.

# WAGON PATTERNS

**TONGUE**
**2**
CUT ONE

**RIM**
**3**
CUT ONE

**HANDLE**
**4**
CUT ONE

**HANDLEBAR**
**5**
CUT ONE

**WAGON BED**
**1**
CUT ONE

**HUBCAPS**
**7**
CUT TWO

**WHEELS**
**6**
CUT TWO

**Materials:** *black, brown, green, red, white and yellow paper; scissors; glue; black crayon or marker*

# SIGNS

**1** Cut one #1 stop sign from red paper. Cut letters from white paper or use a marker to write *STOP* on the sign. Cut one #7 post from brown paper and glue to the bottom of the back side of the sign.

**2** Cut one #2 body from black paper. Cut three #3 lights, one each from red, yellow and green paper. Glue to the body as shown. Cut one #7 post from brown paper and glue to the bottom of the back side of the sign.

**3** Cut one #4 yield sign from yellow paper. Cut letters from black paper or use a marker to write *Yield* on the sign. Cut one #7 post from brown paper and glue to the bottom of the back side of the sign.

**4** Cut one #5 railroad sign from yellow paper. Cut two #6 crossbars from black paper and glue in an *X* on the sign. Cut letters from black paper or use a marker to write *R R* on the sign. Cut one #7 post from brown paper and glue to the bottom of the back side of the sign.

**STOP SIGN**

**1**

**CUT ONE**

**POST**

**7**

**CUT ONE**

STOP

**LIGHTS**

**3**

**CUT THREE**

**BODY**

**2**

**CUT ONE**

**CROSSBARS**

**6**

**CUT TWO**

# Yield

**YIELD SIGN**

**4**

**CUT ONE**

**RAILROAD SIGN**

**5**

**CUT ONE**

R    R